a Boy Like ME

A Wordless Picture Book

Stephanie O'Connor

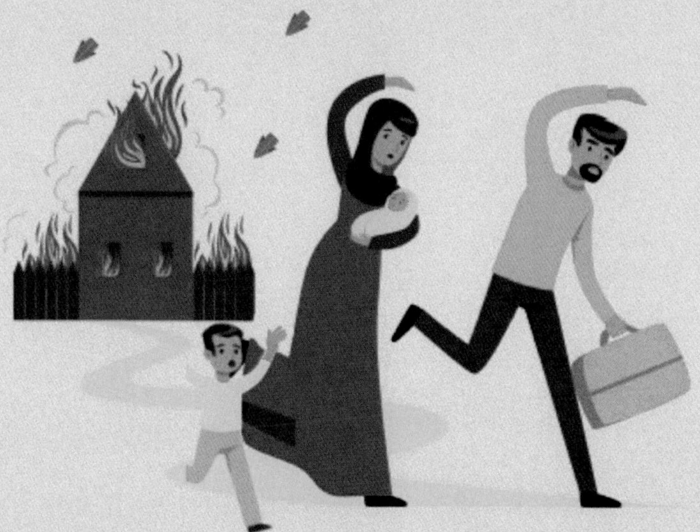

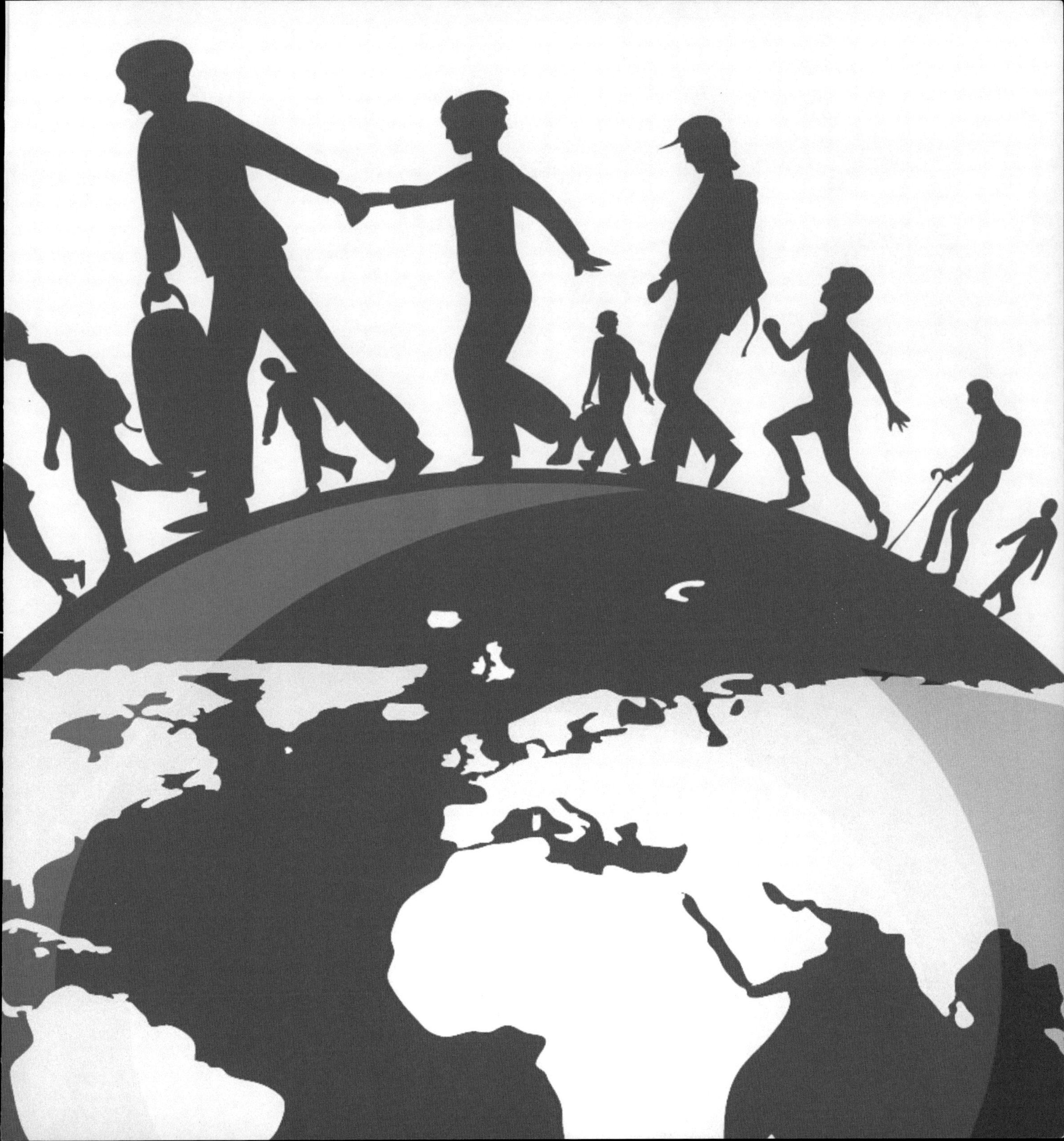

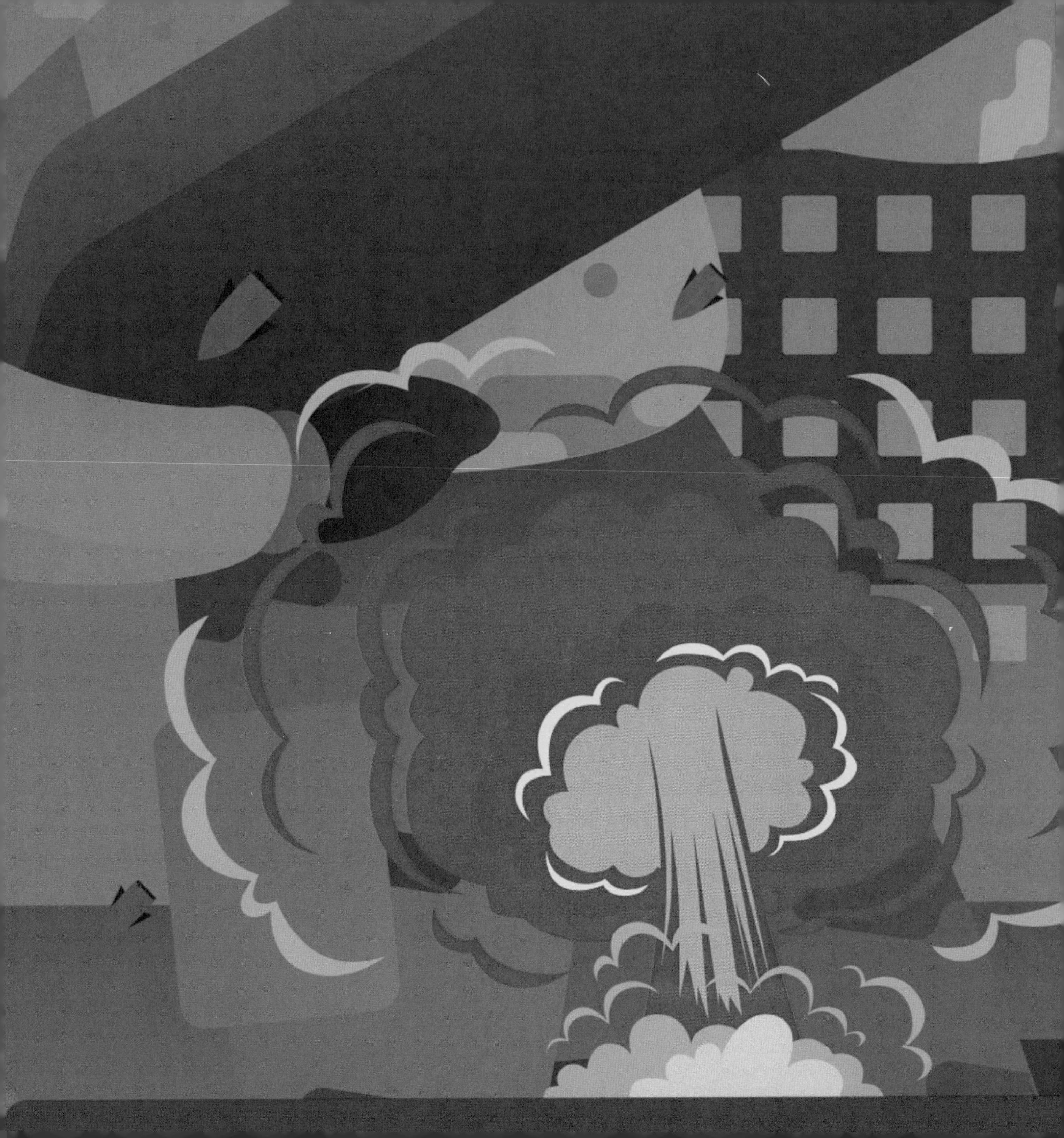

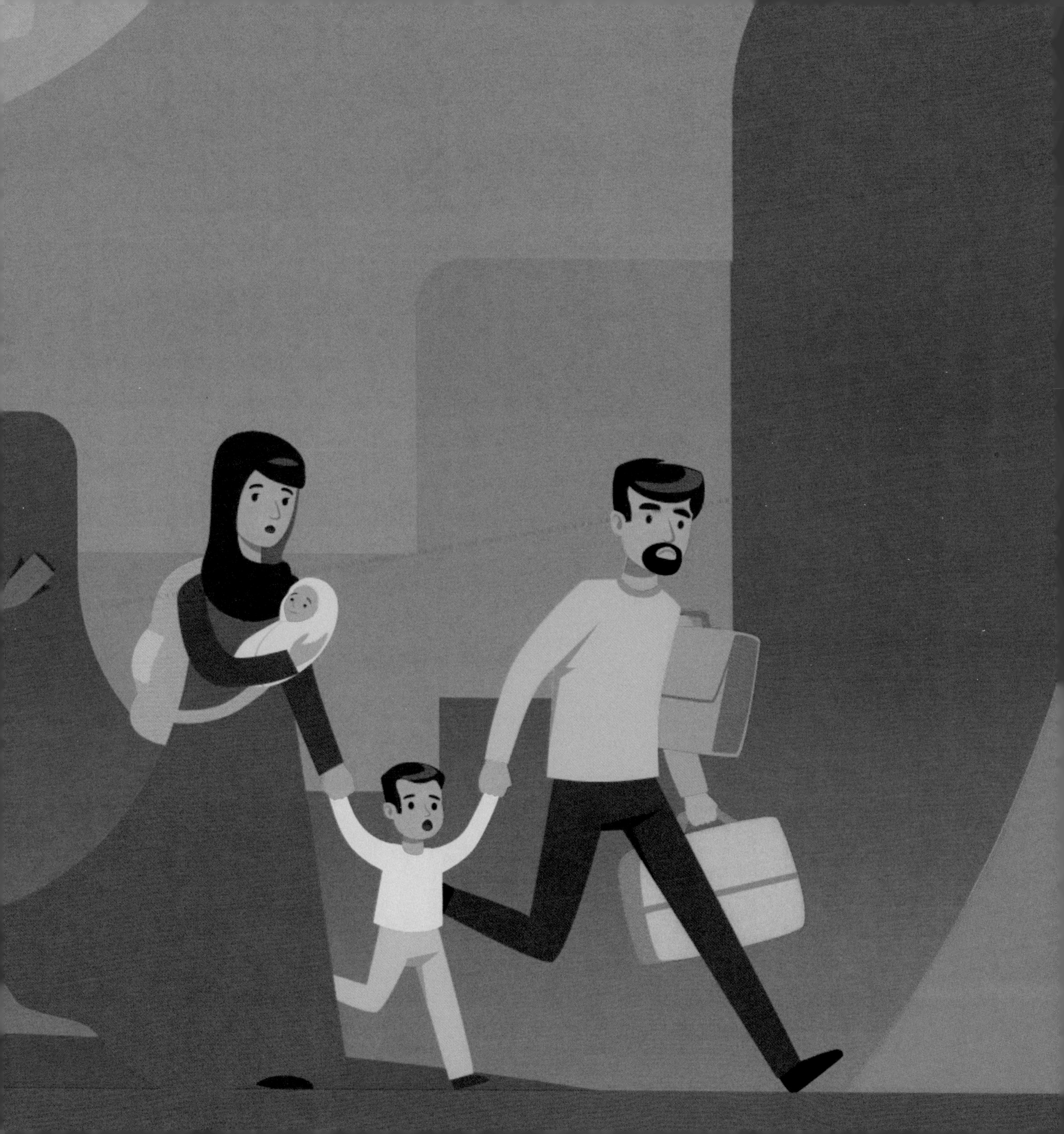

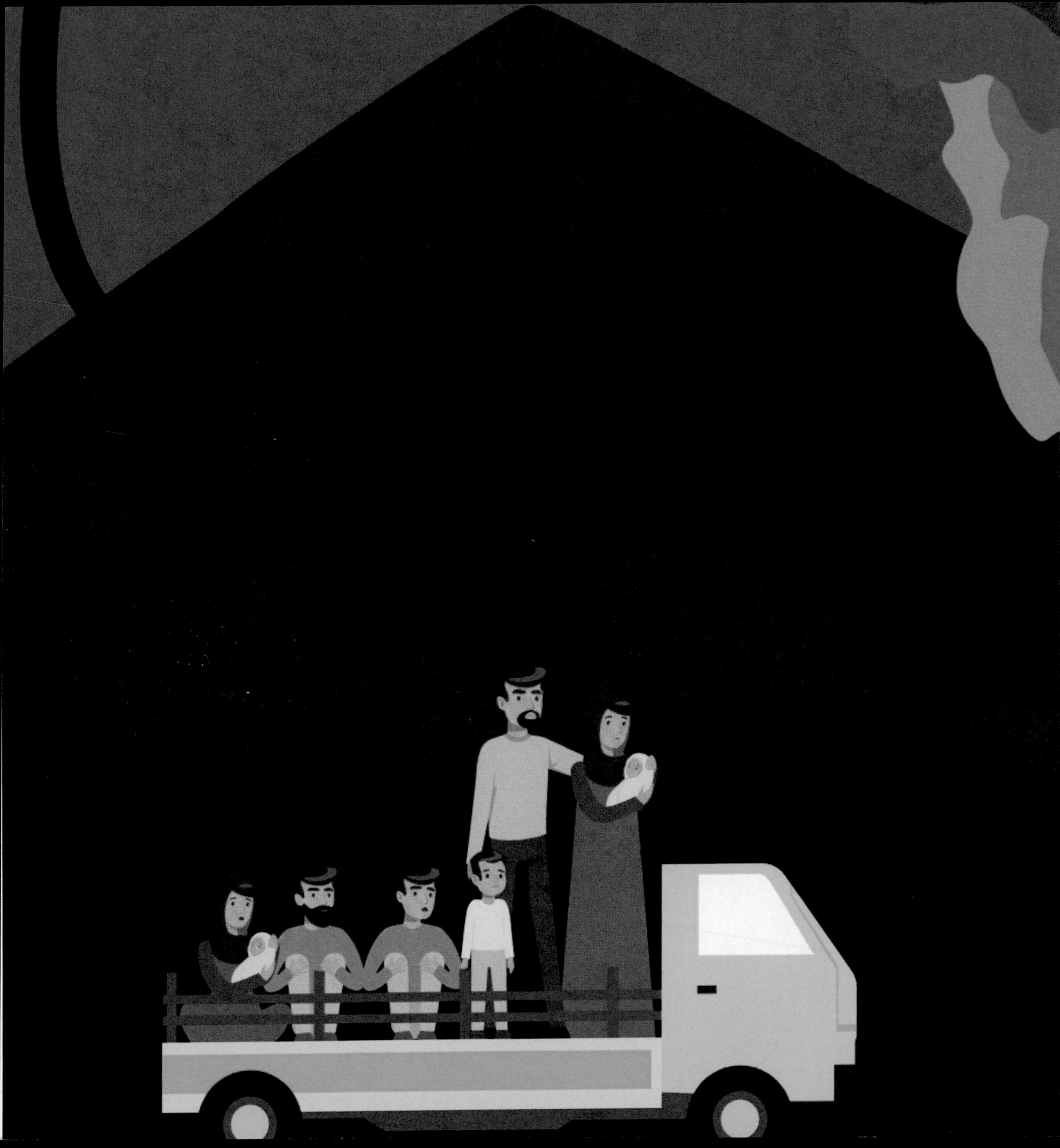

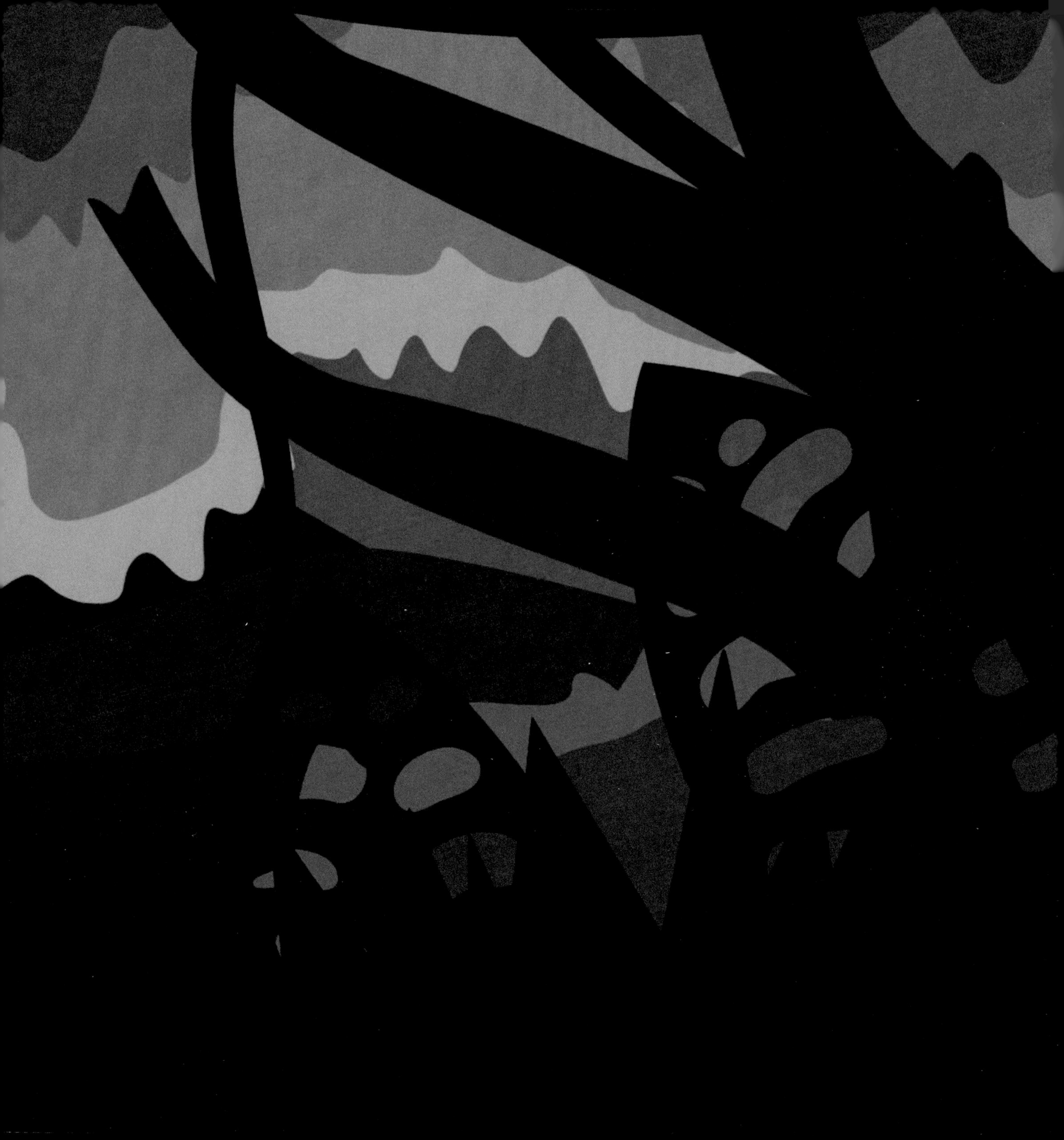

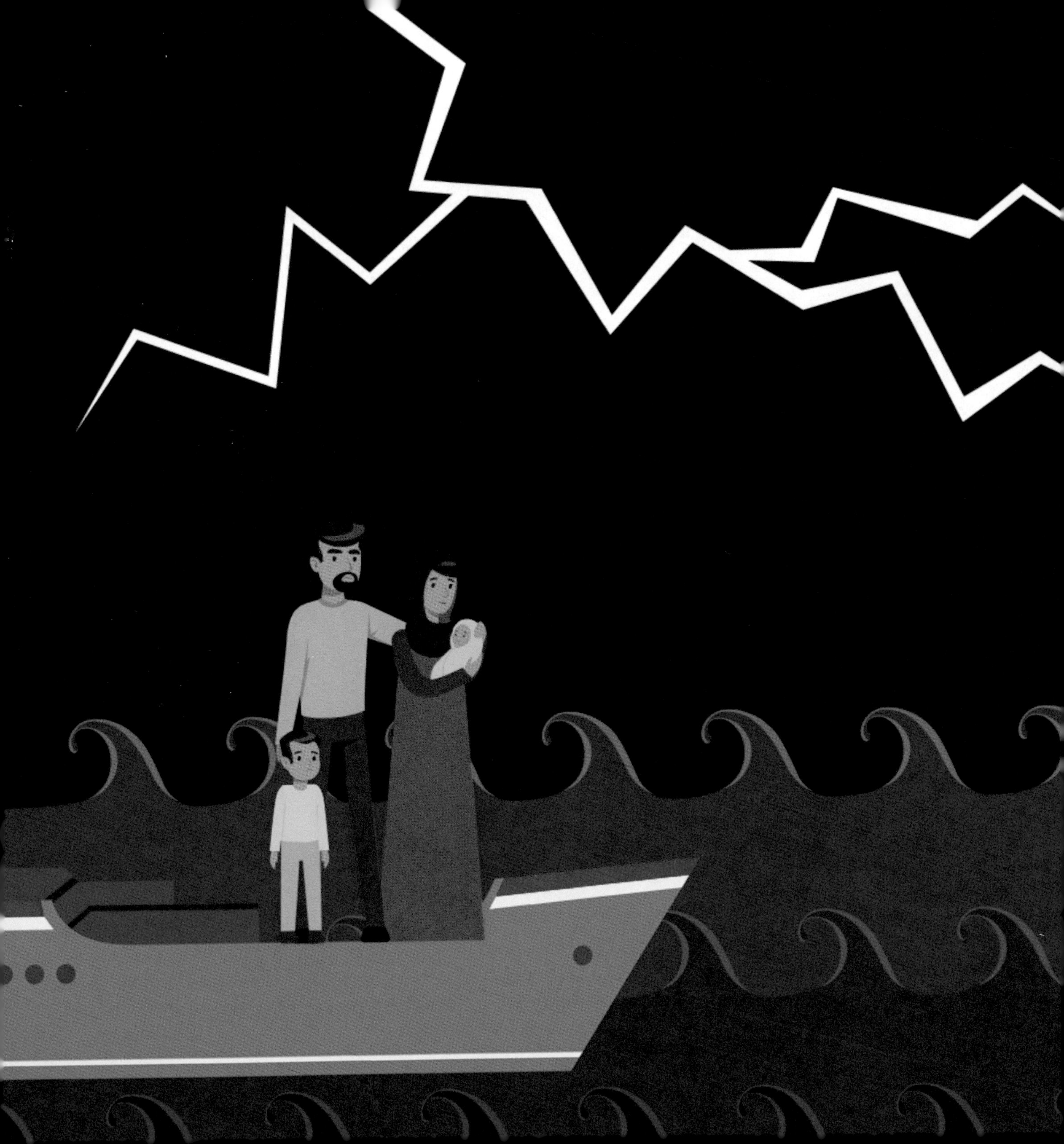

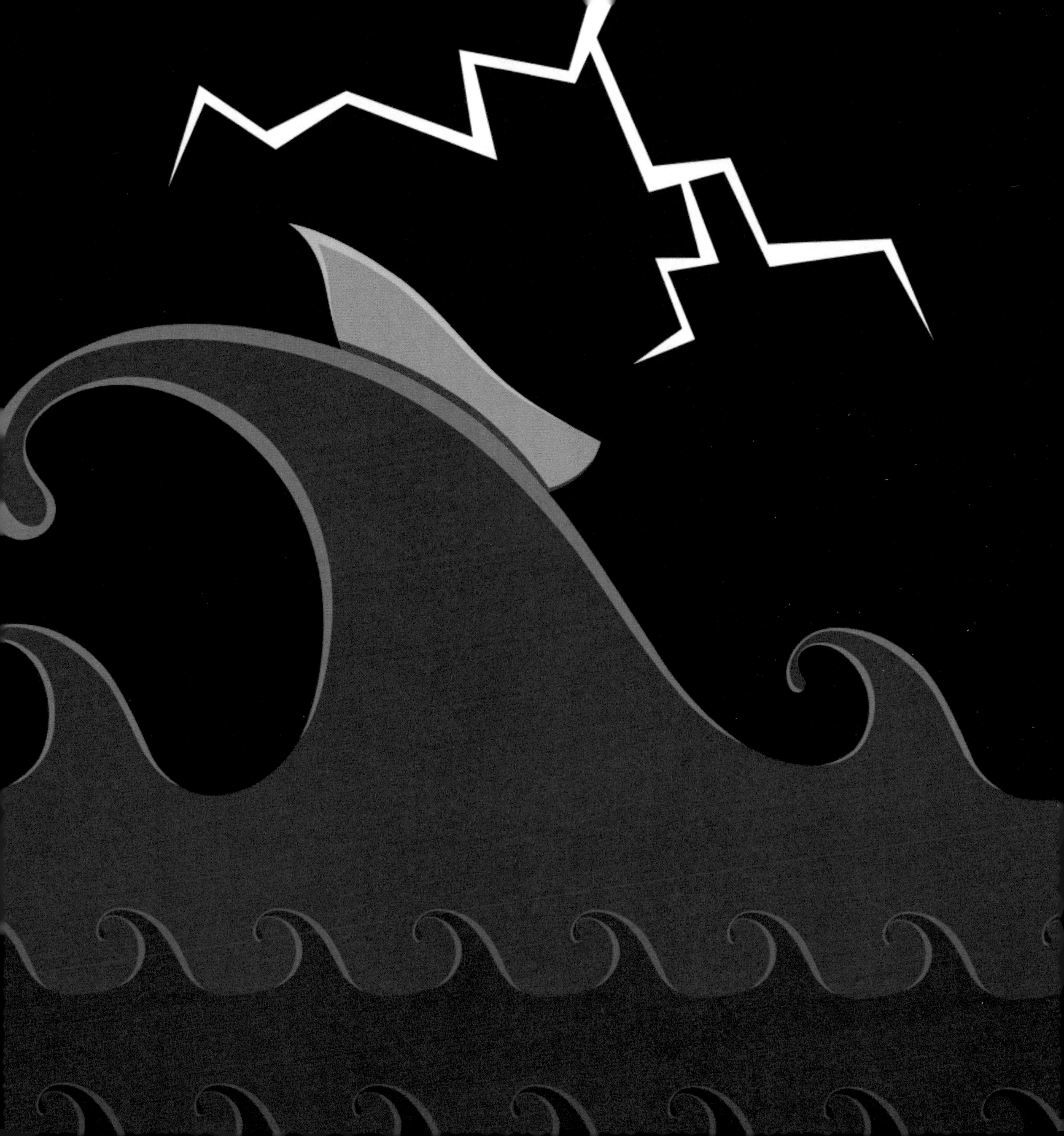

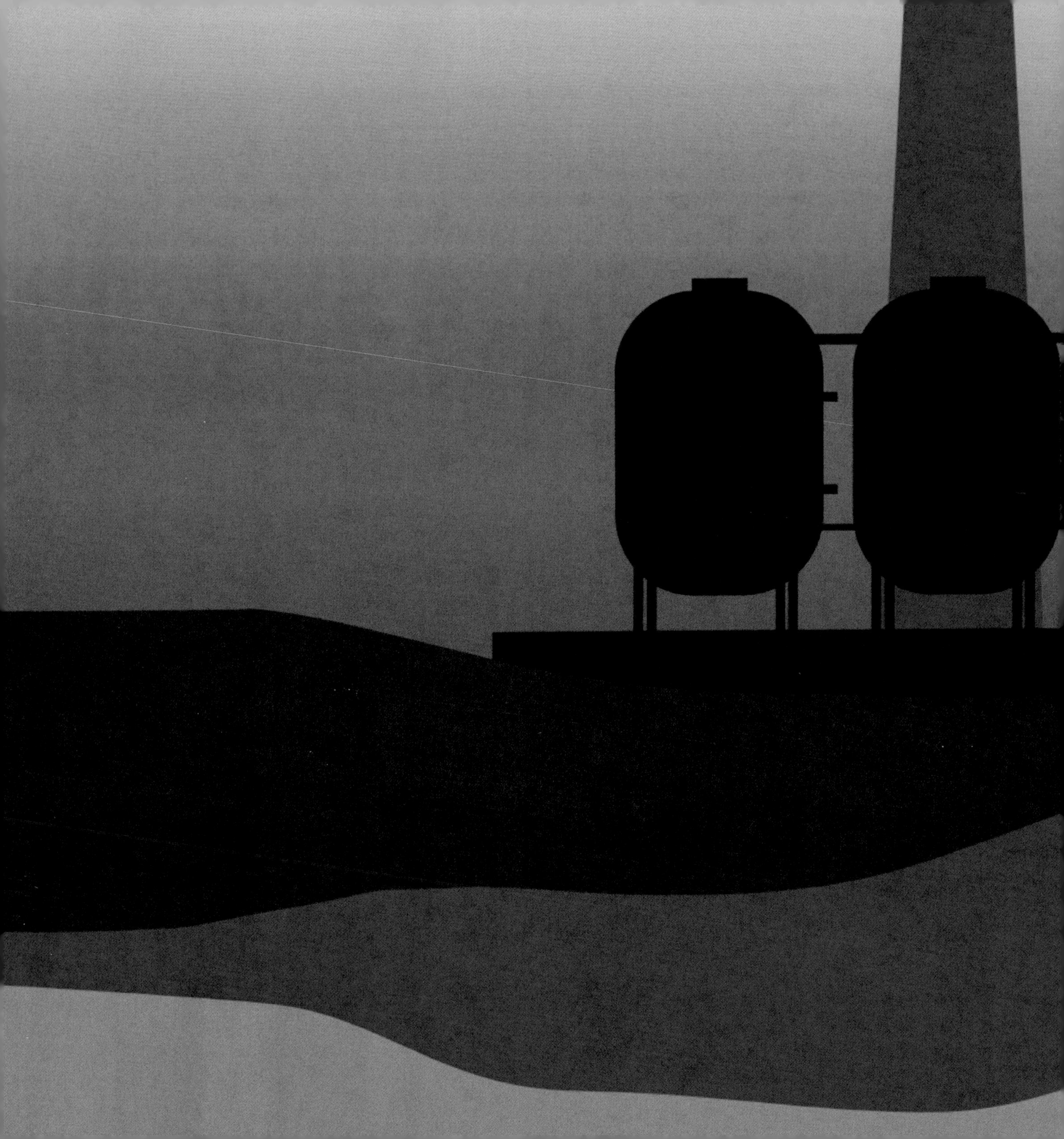

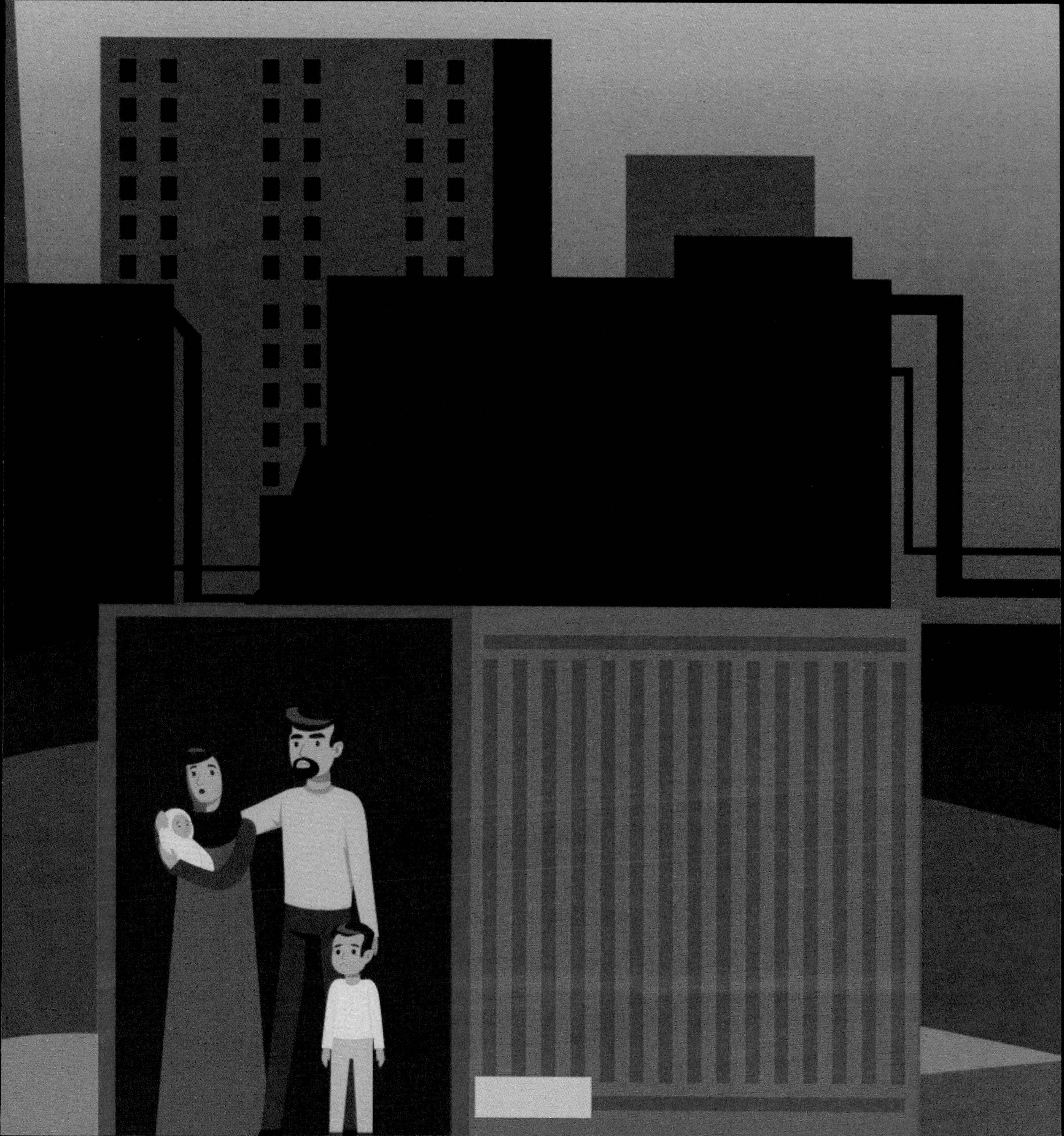

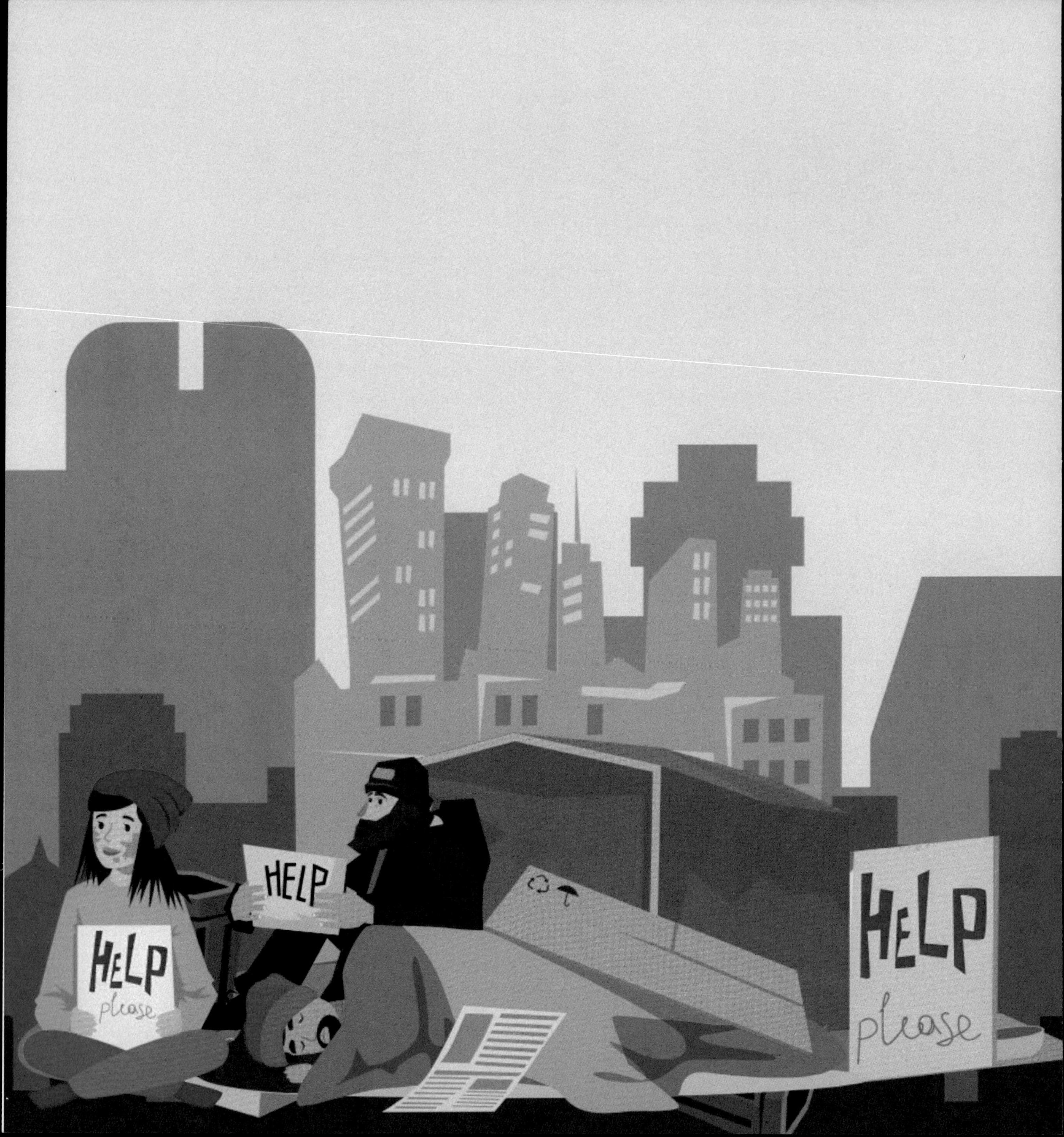
HELP
HELP
please
HELP
please

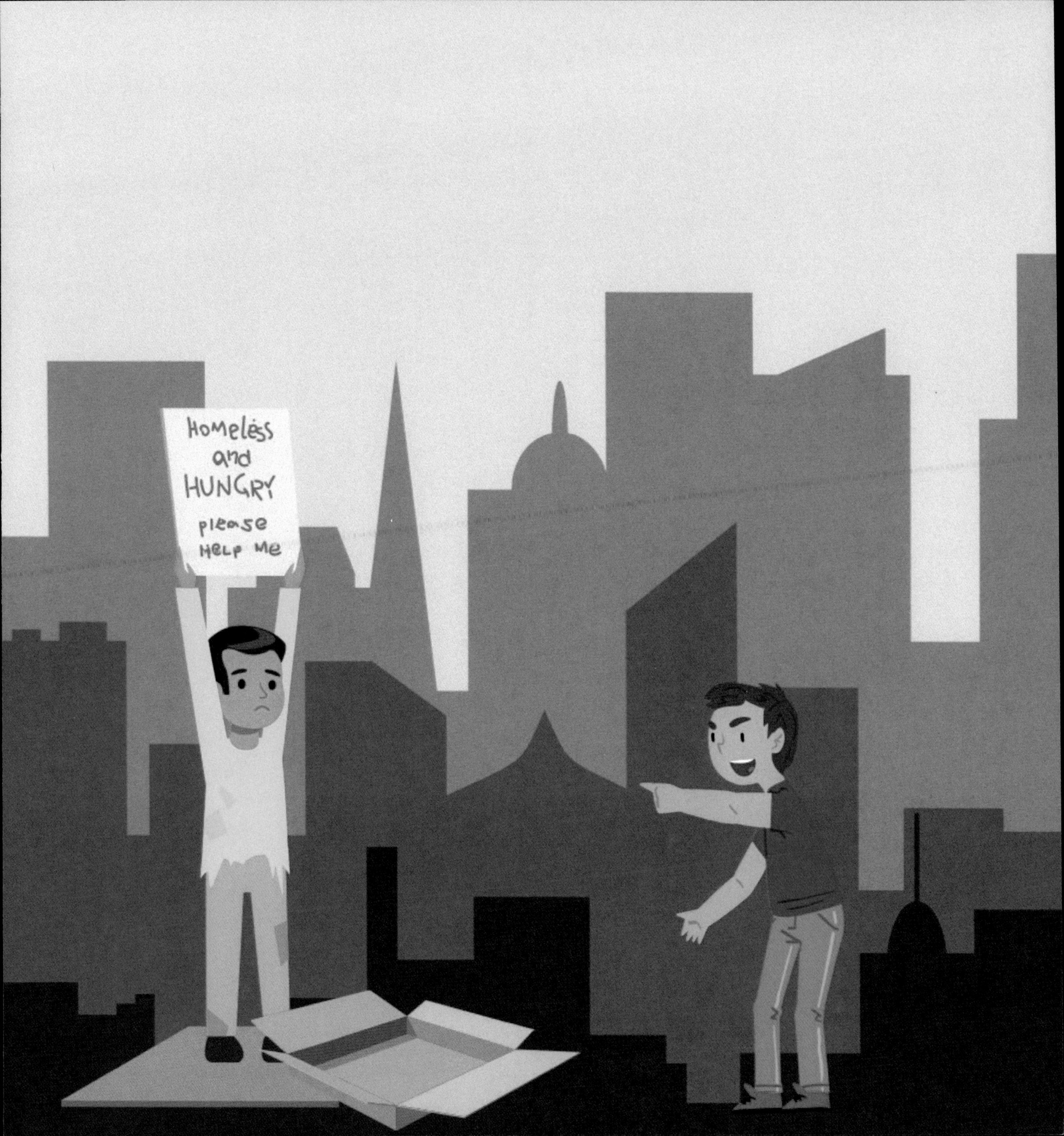
Homeless
and
HUNGRY
please
Help me

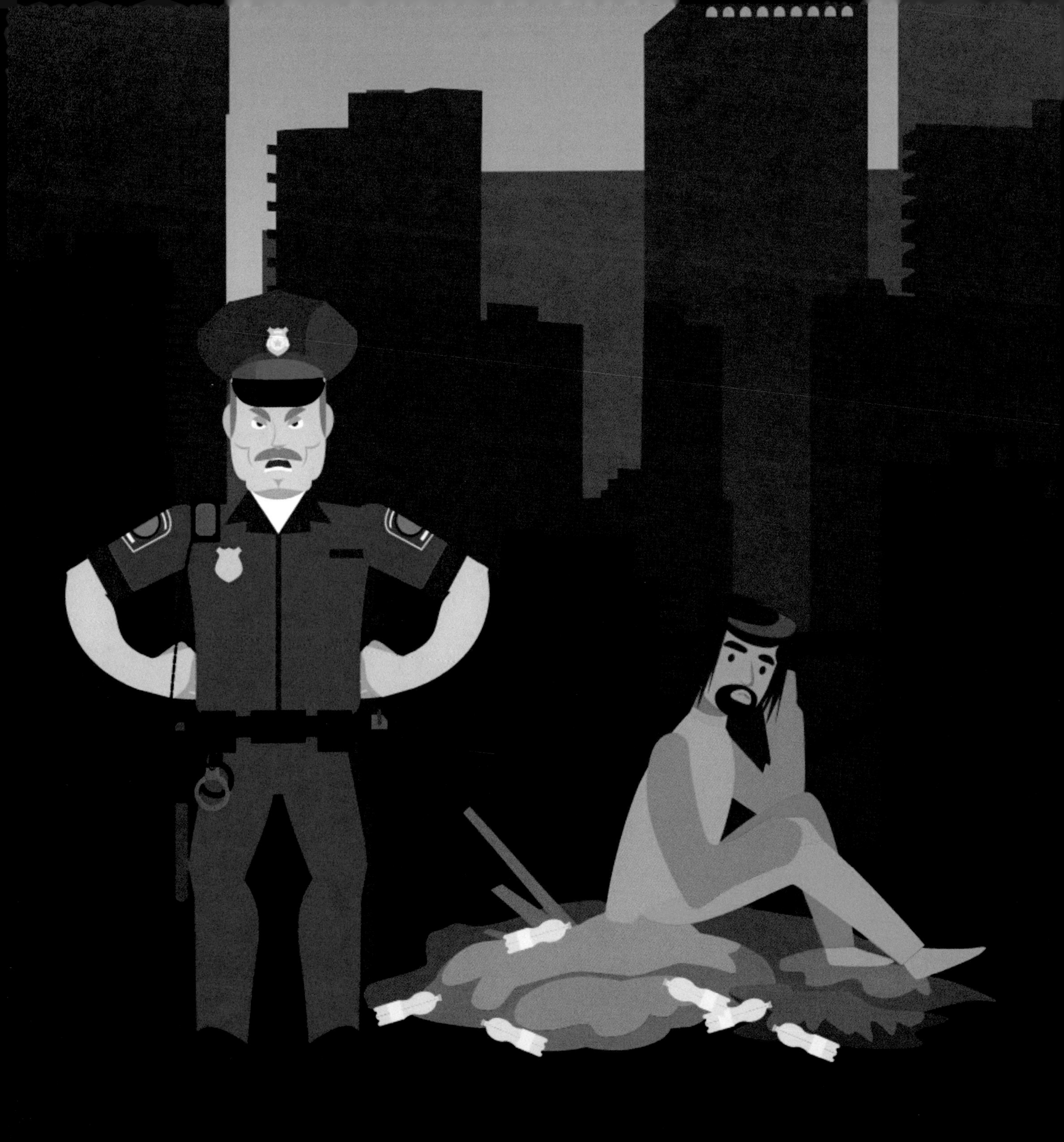

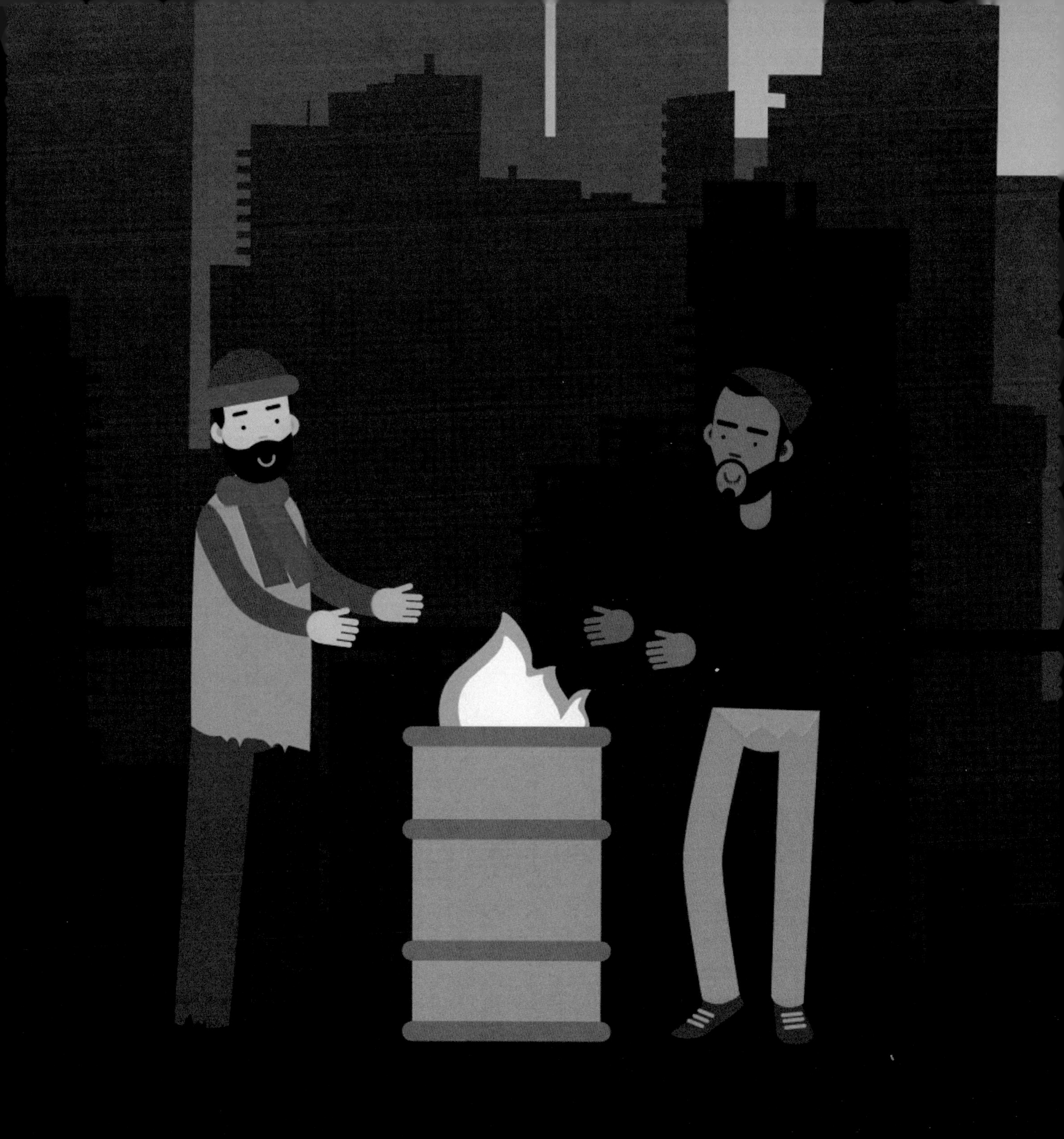

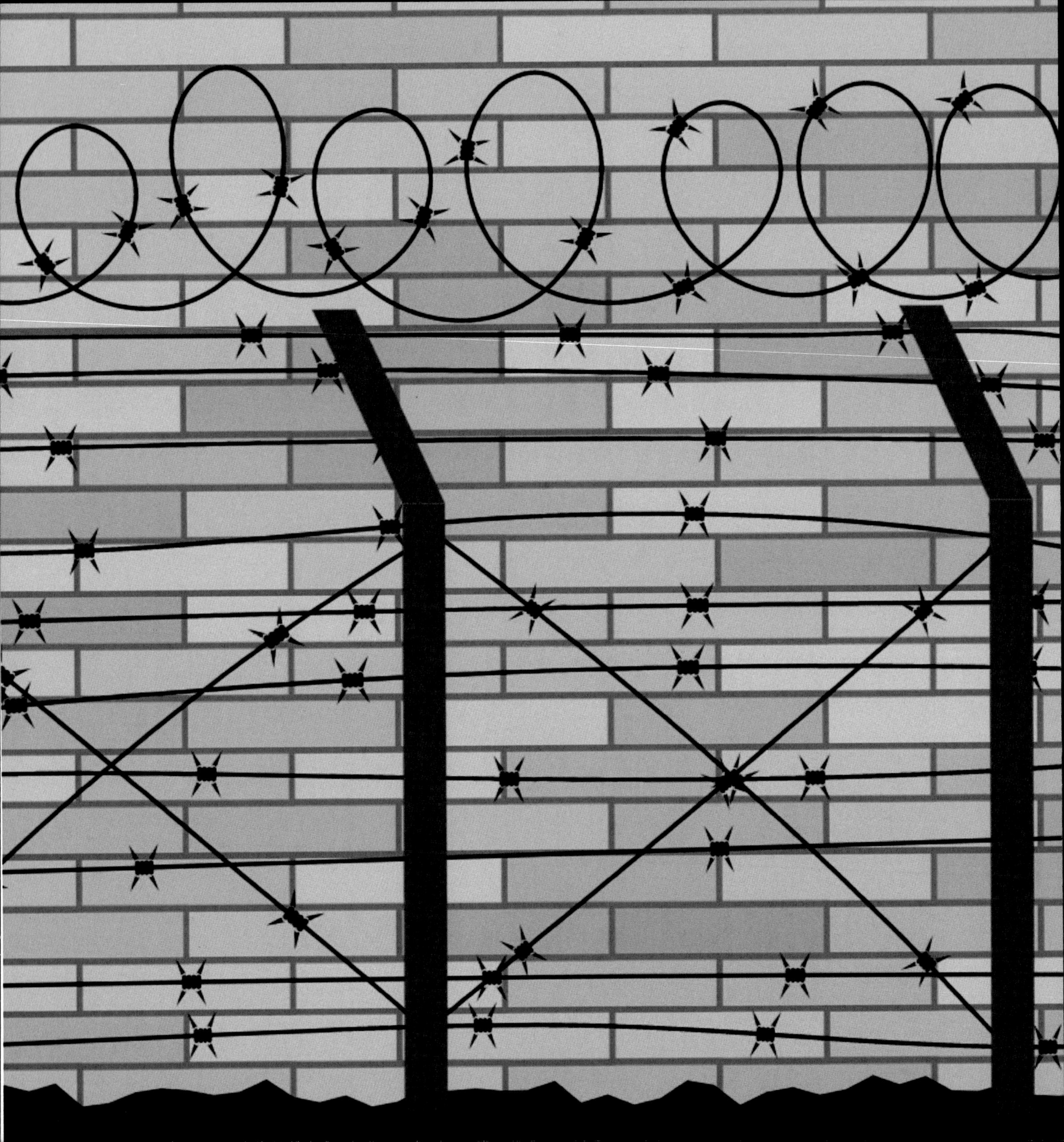

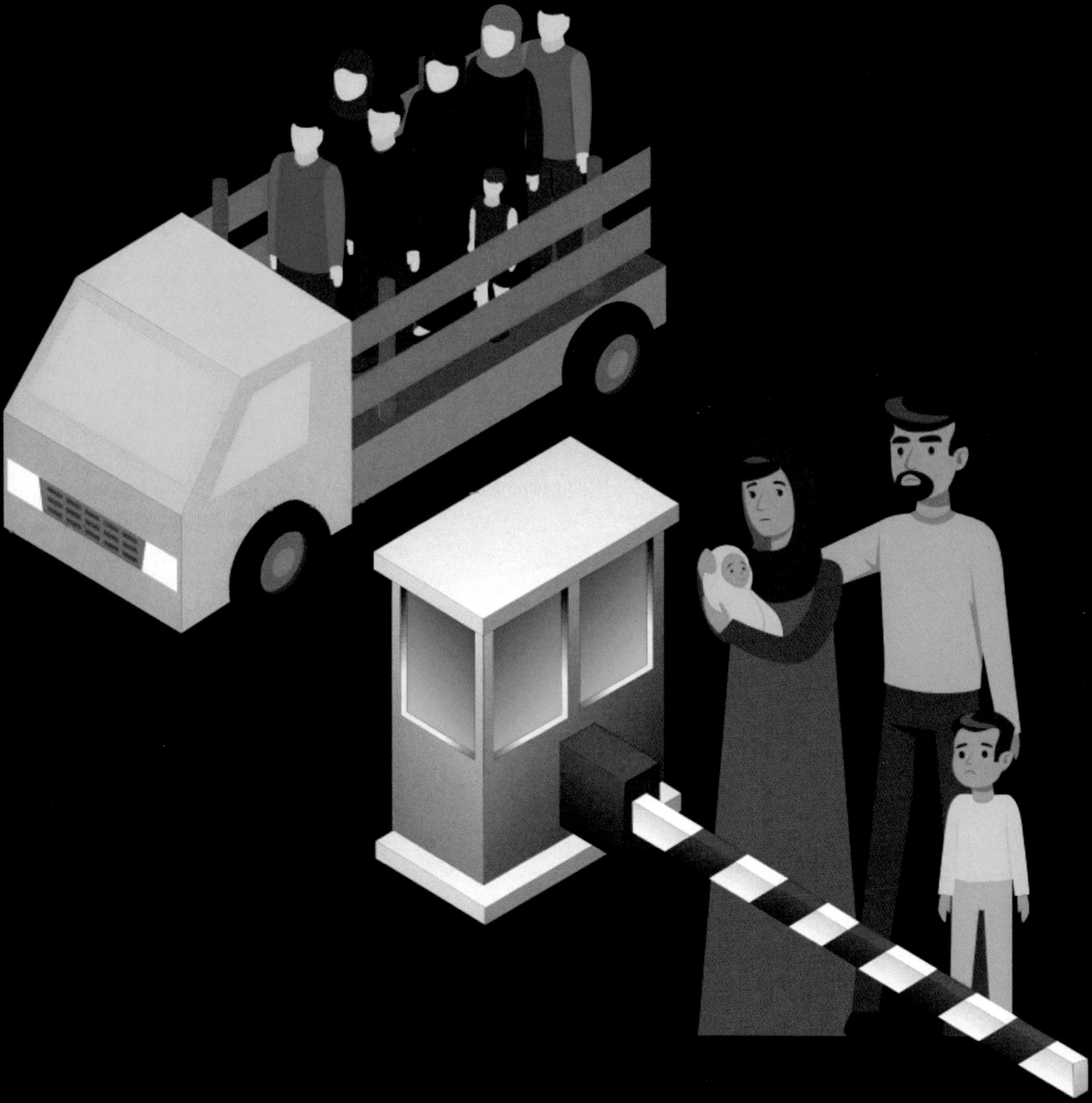

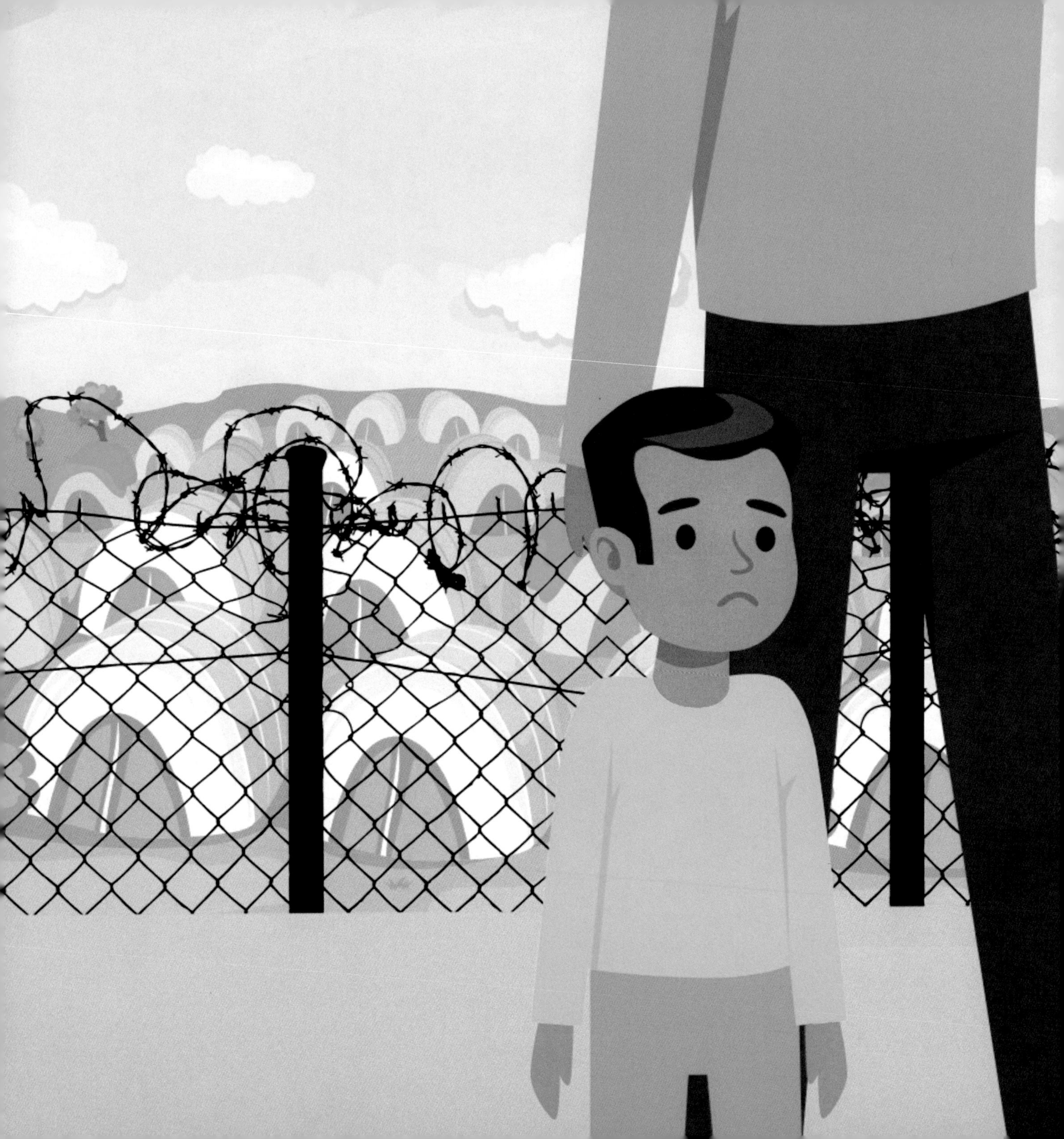

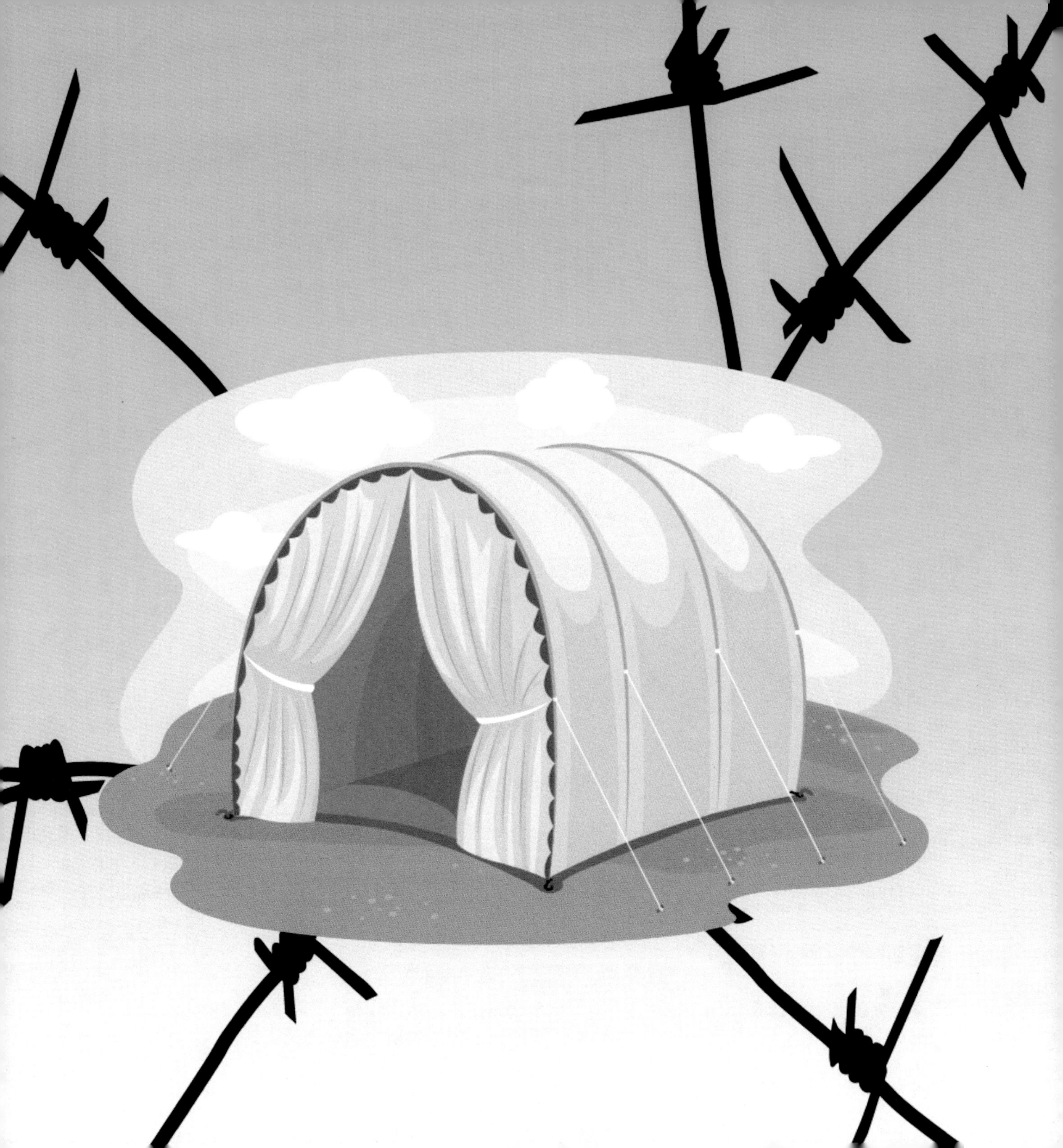

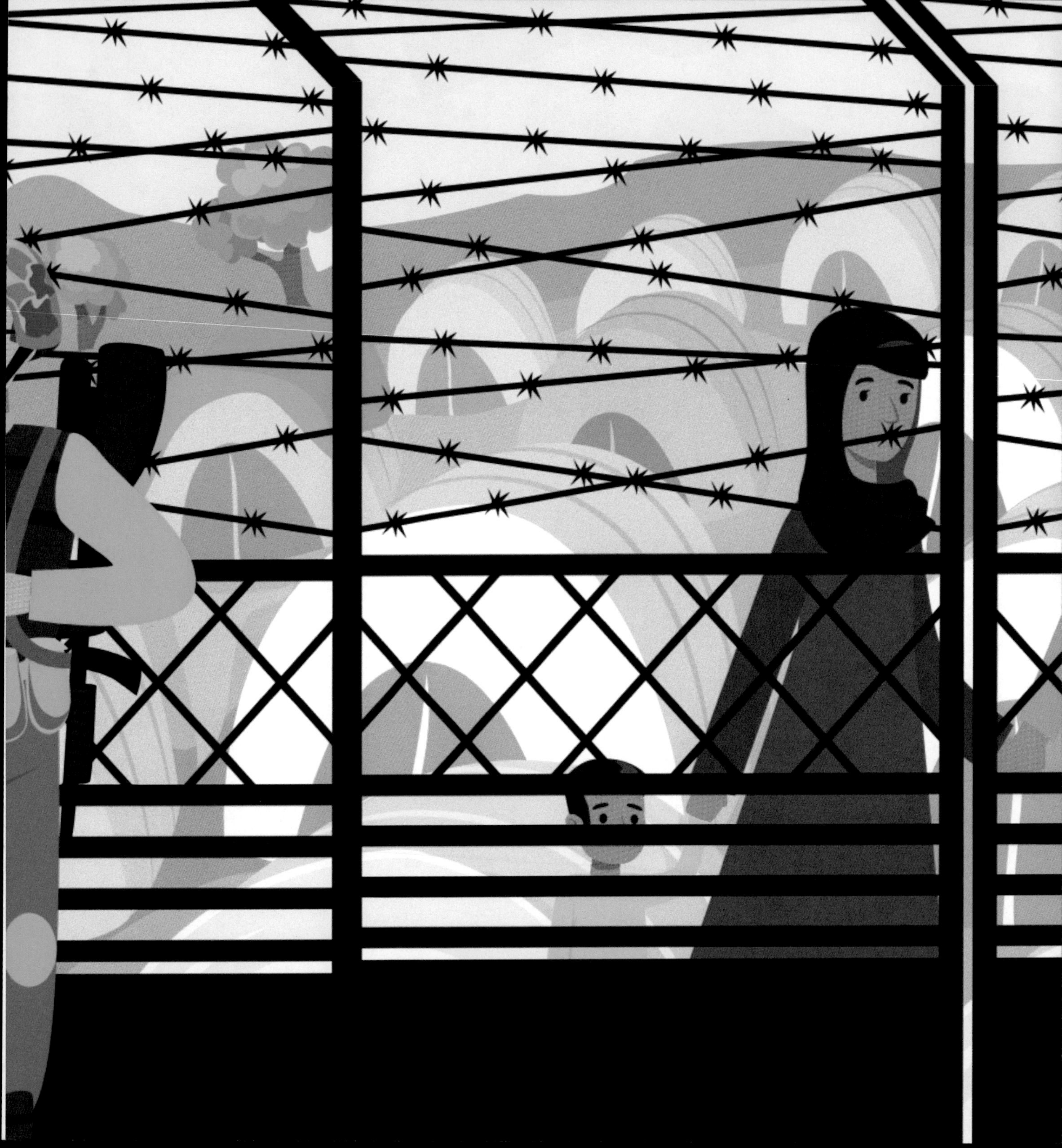

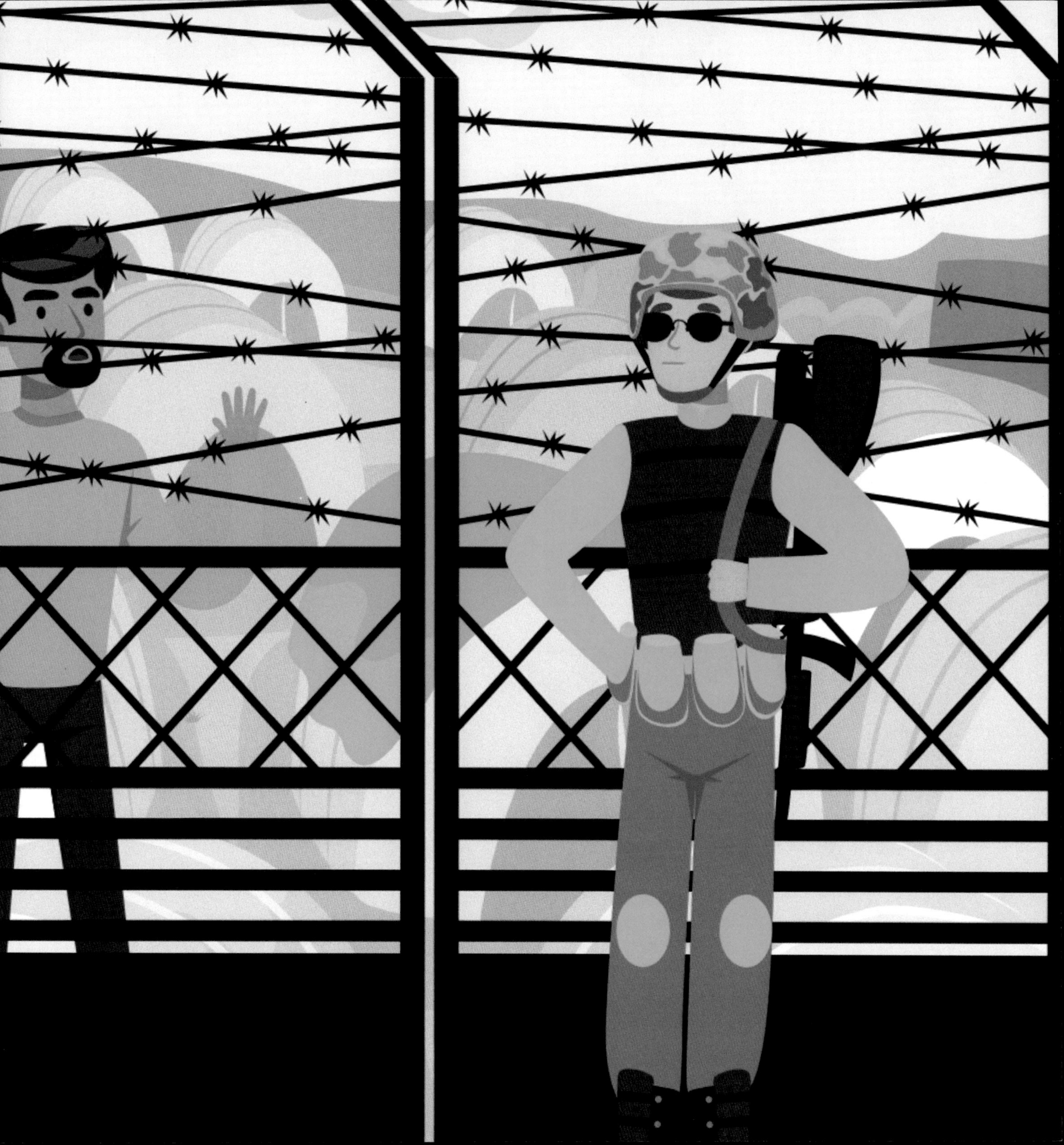

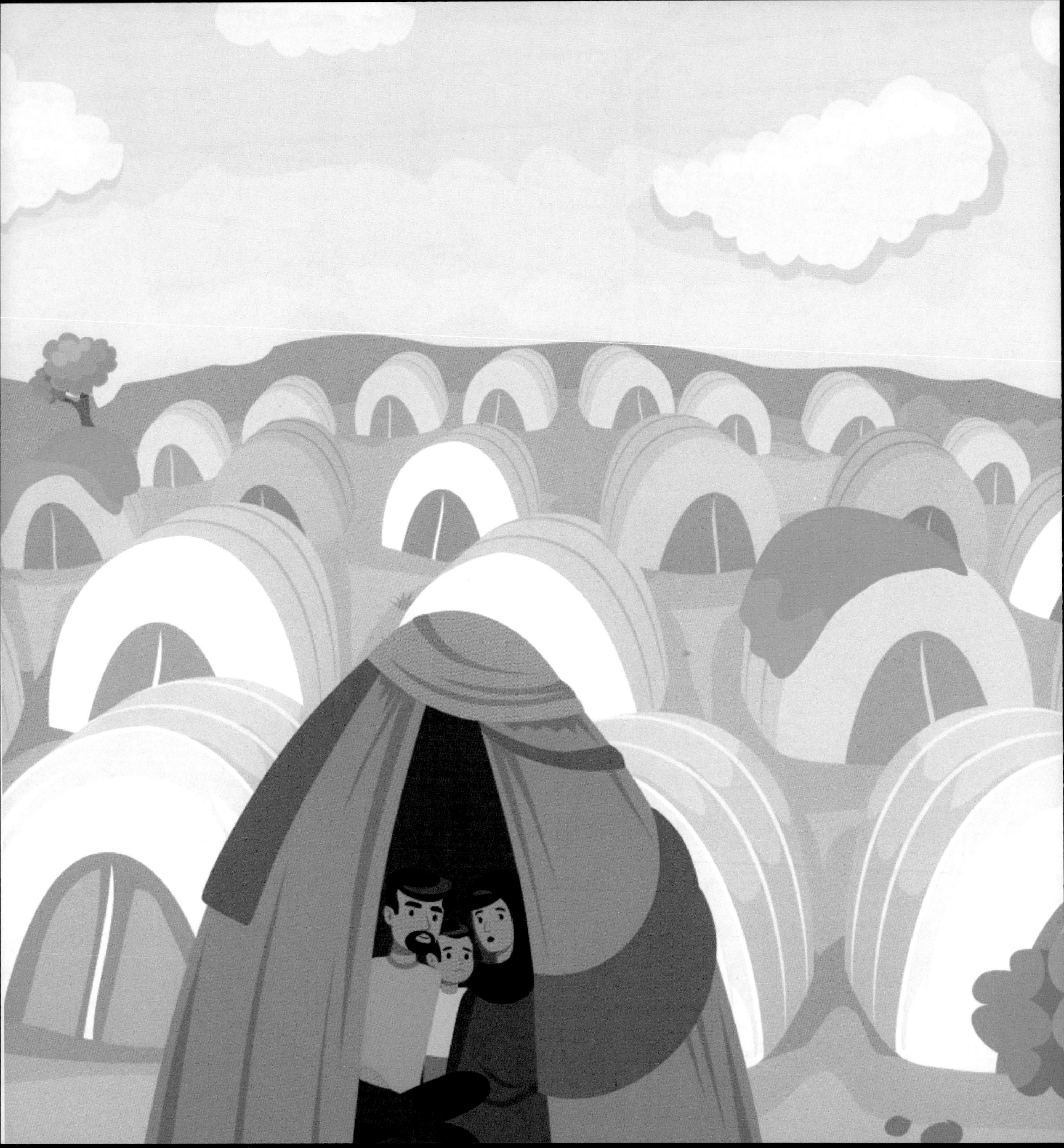

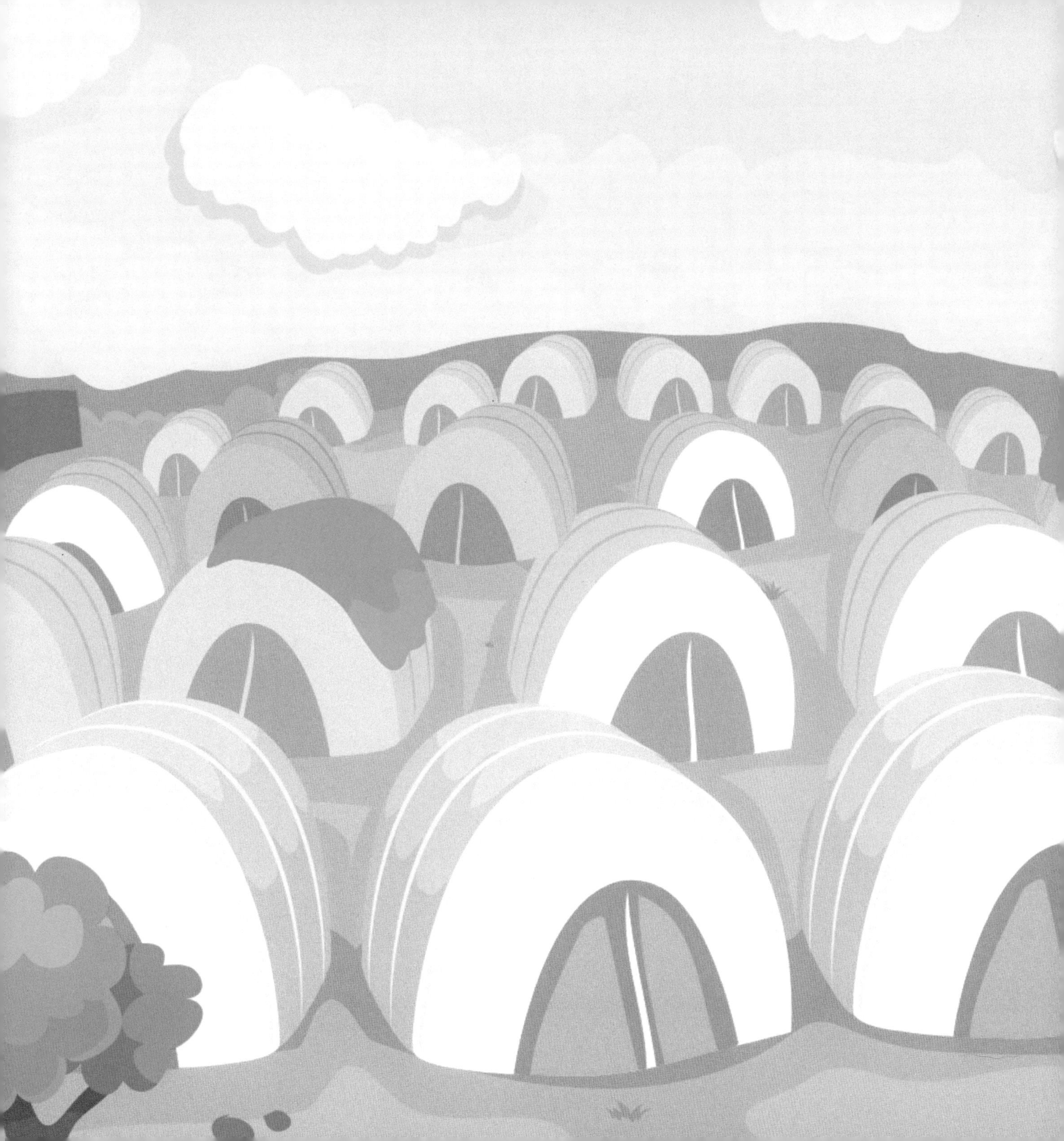

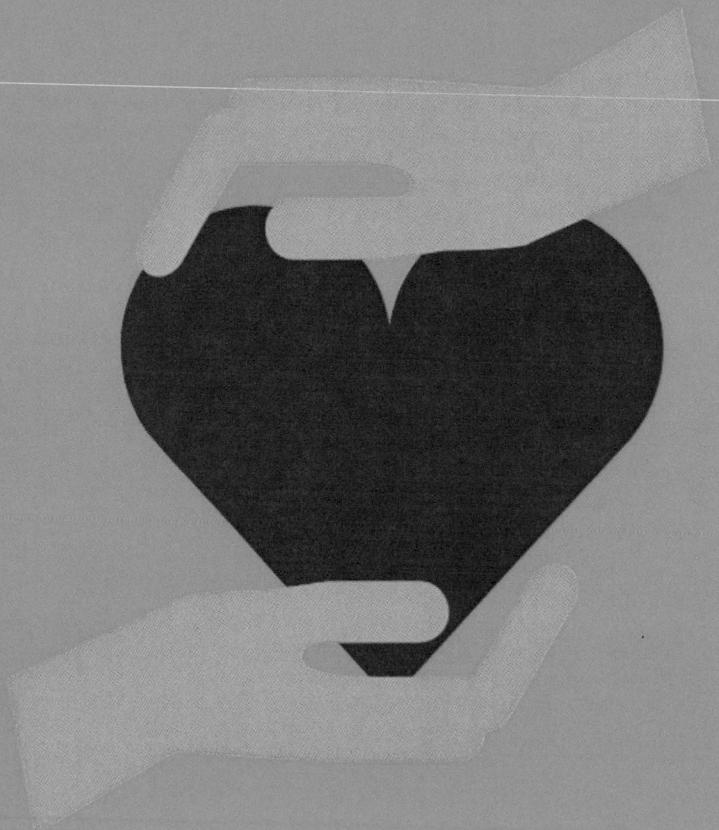

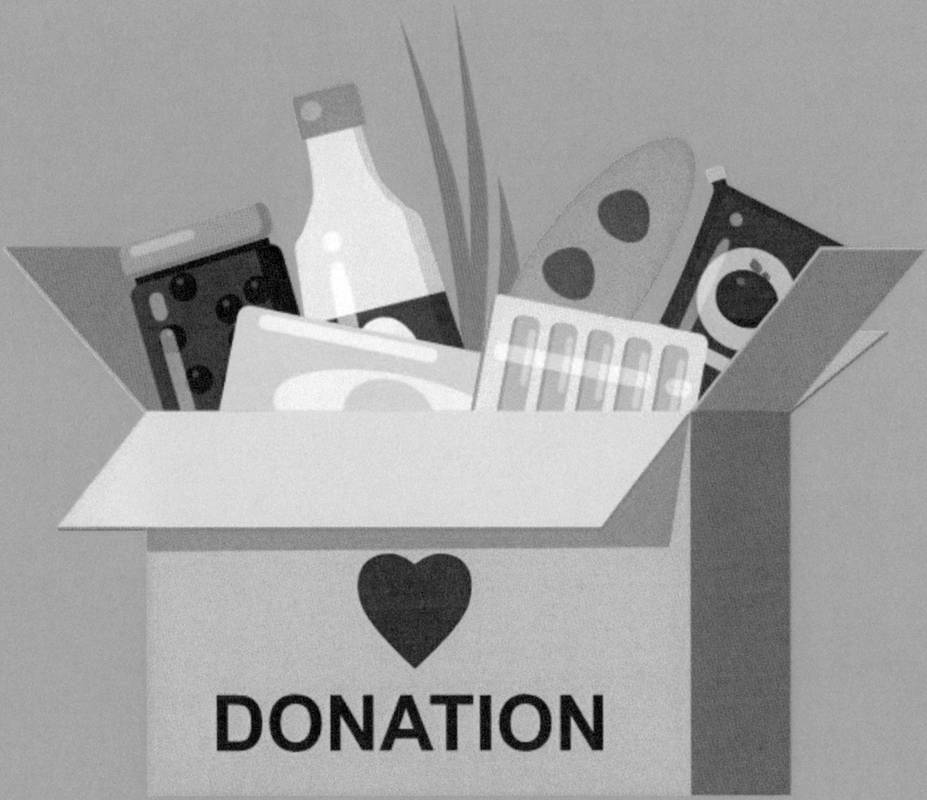
DONATION

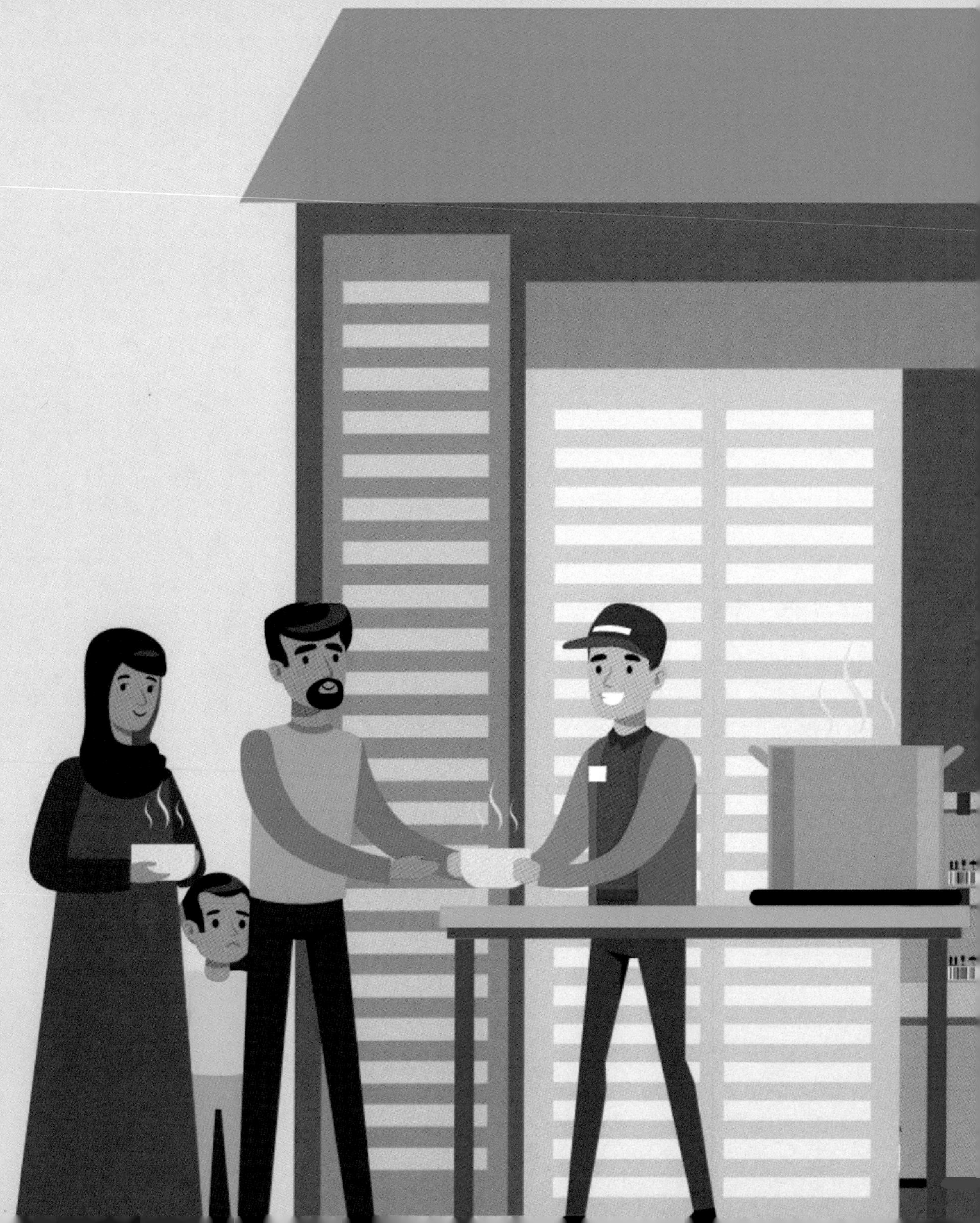

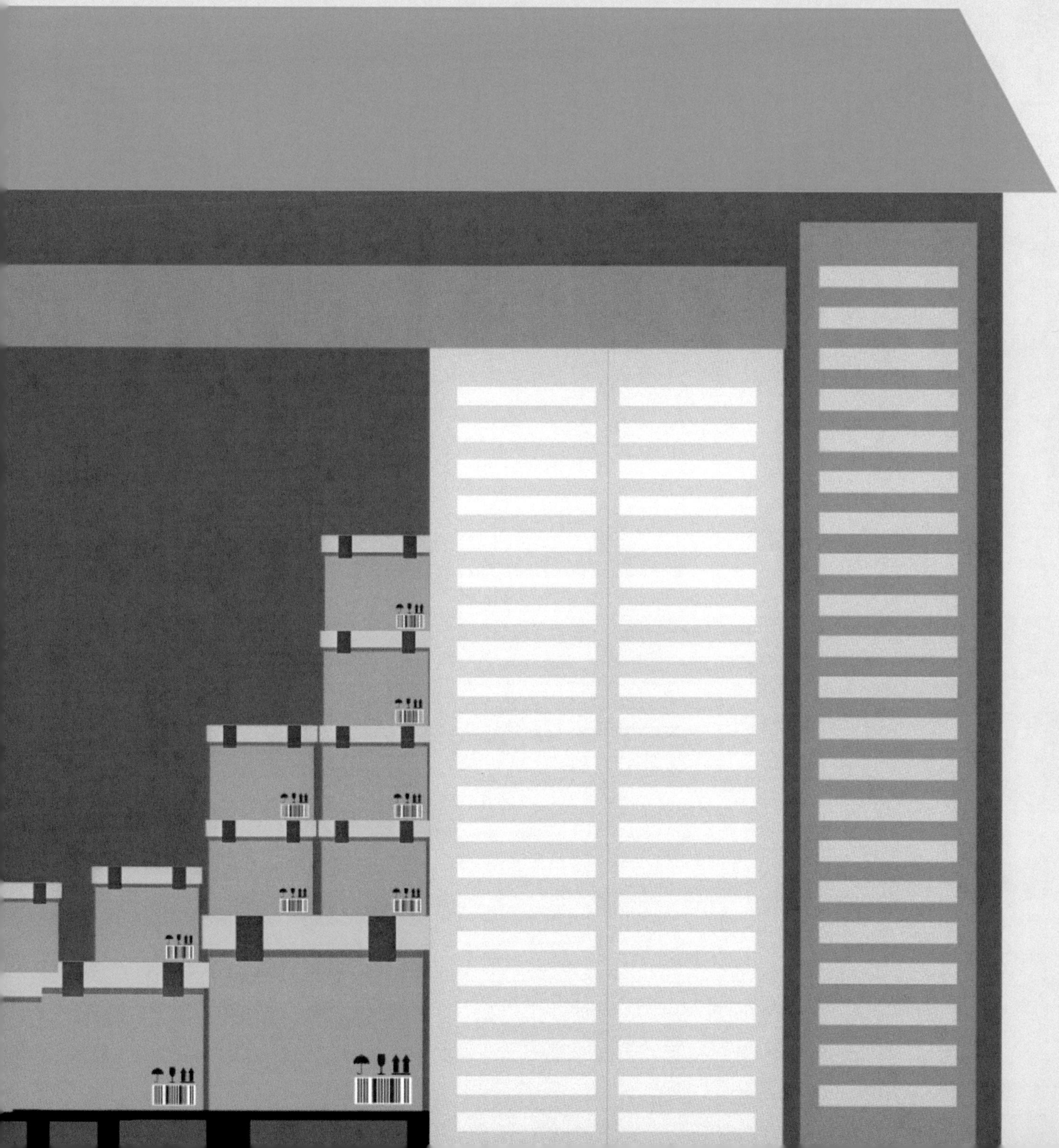

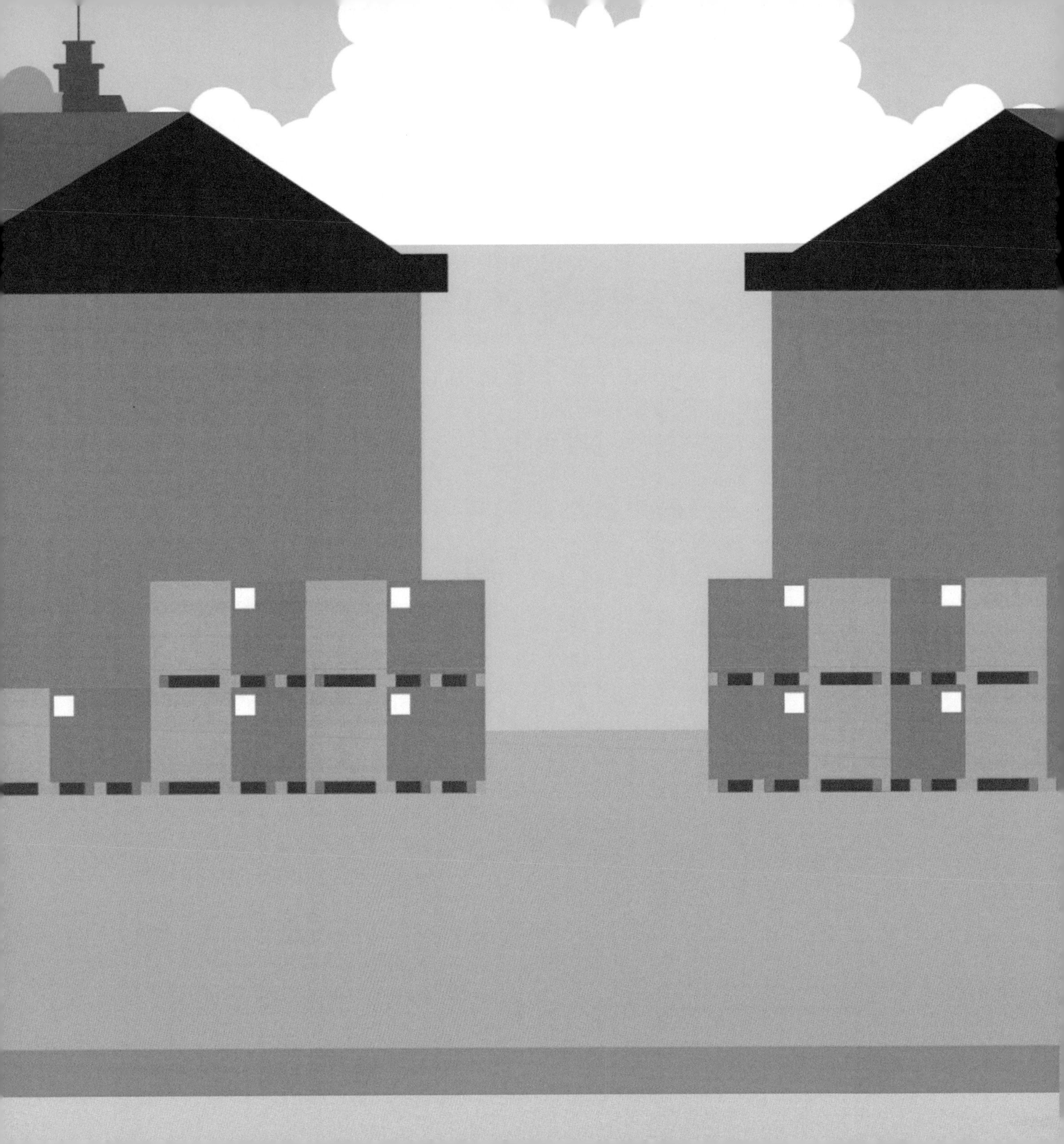

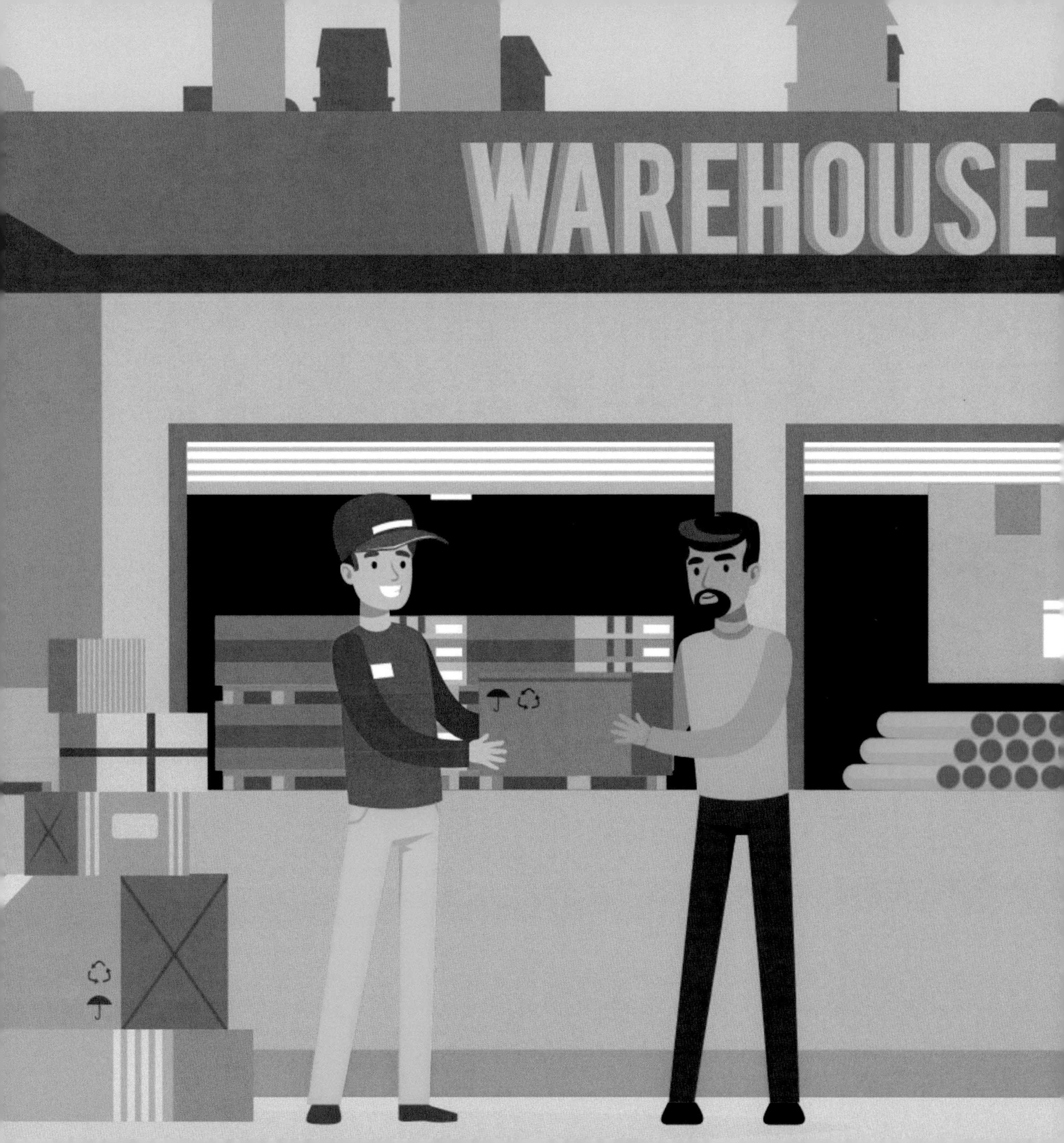
WAREHOUSE

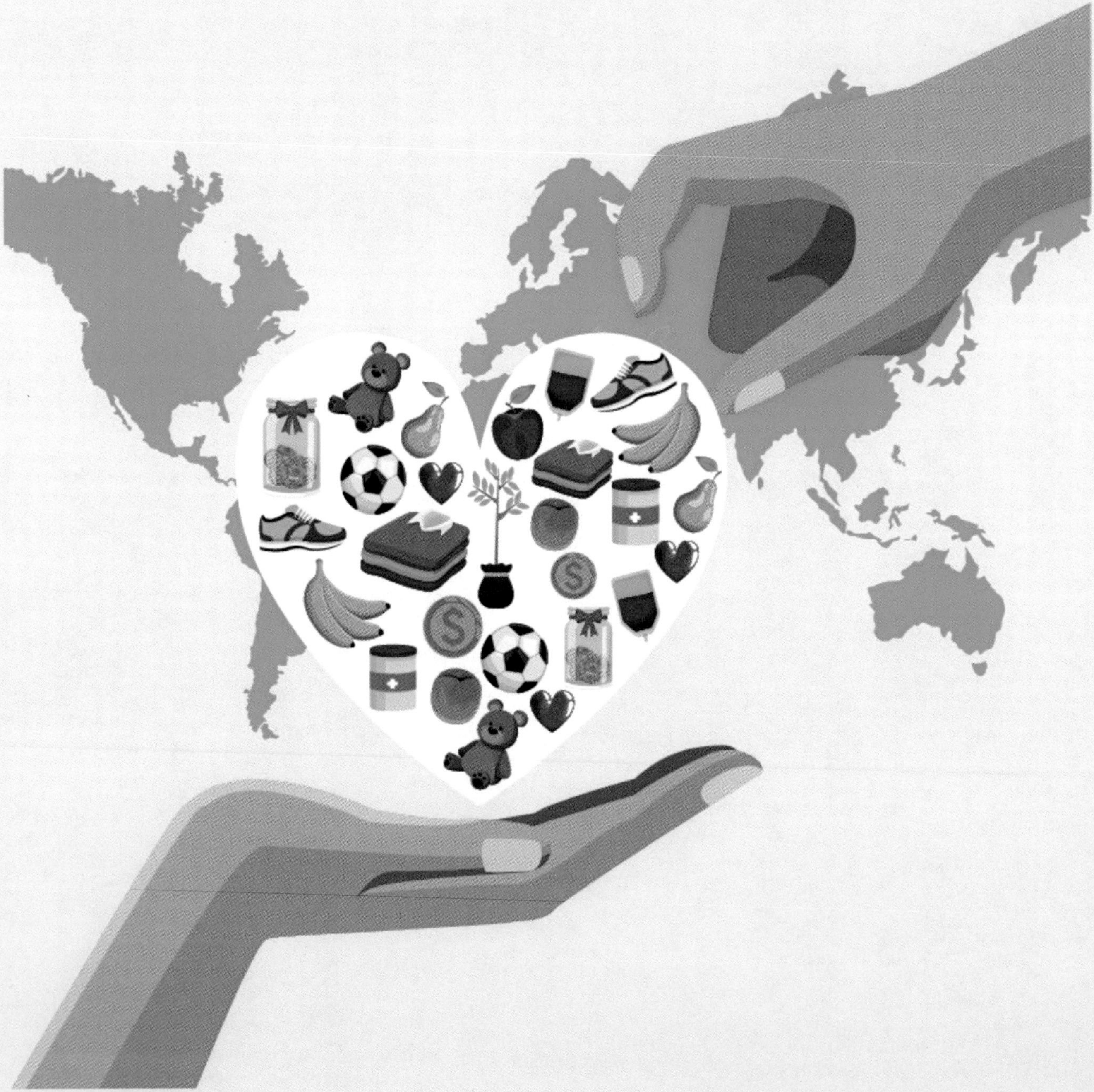

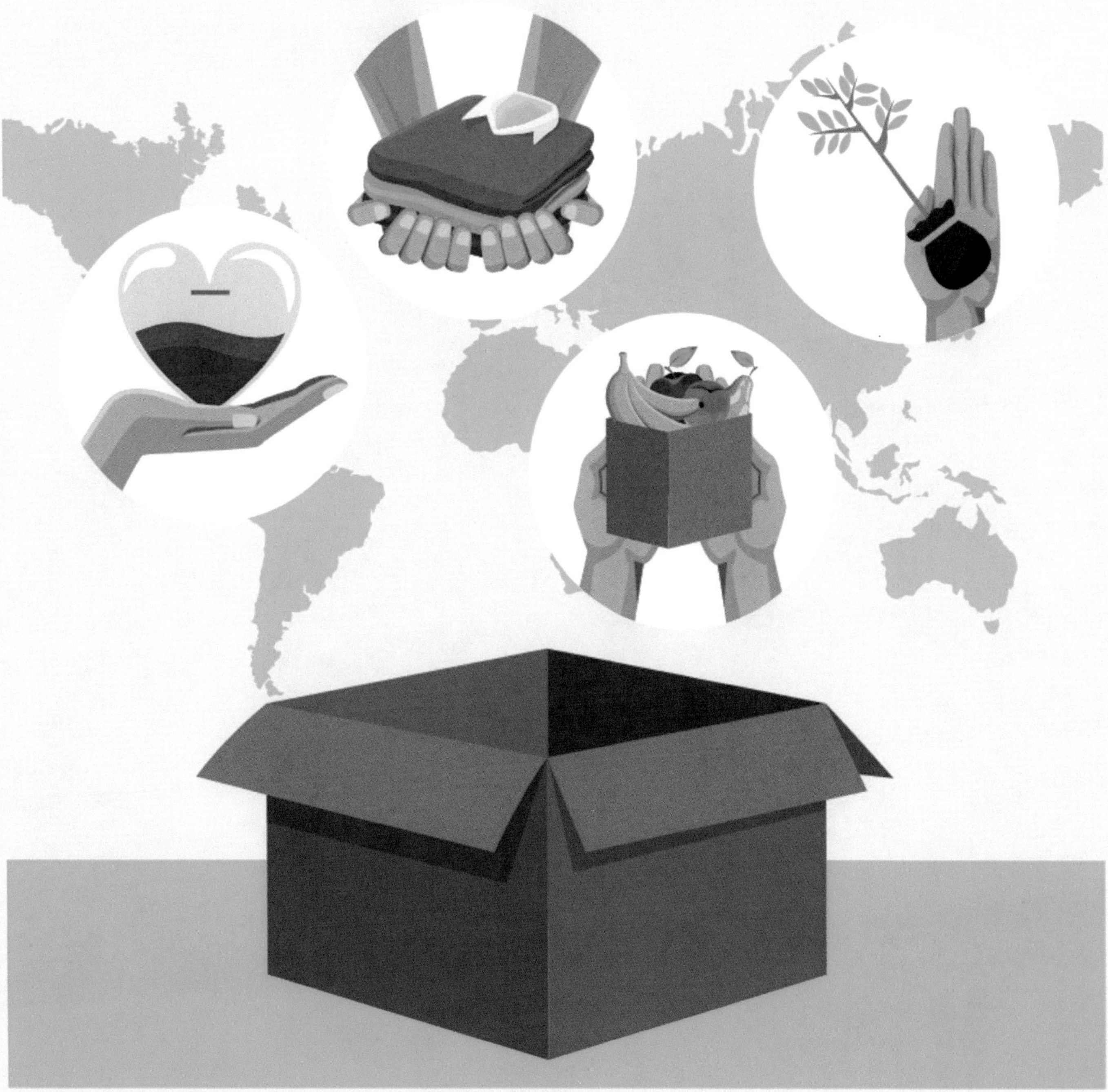

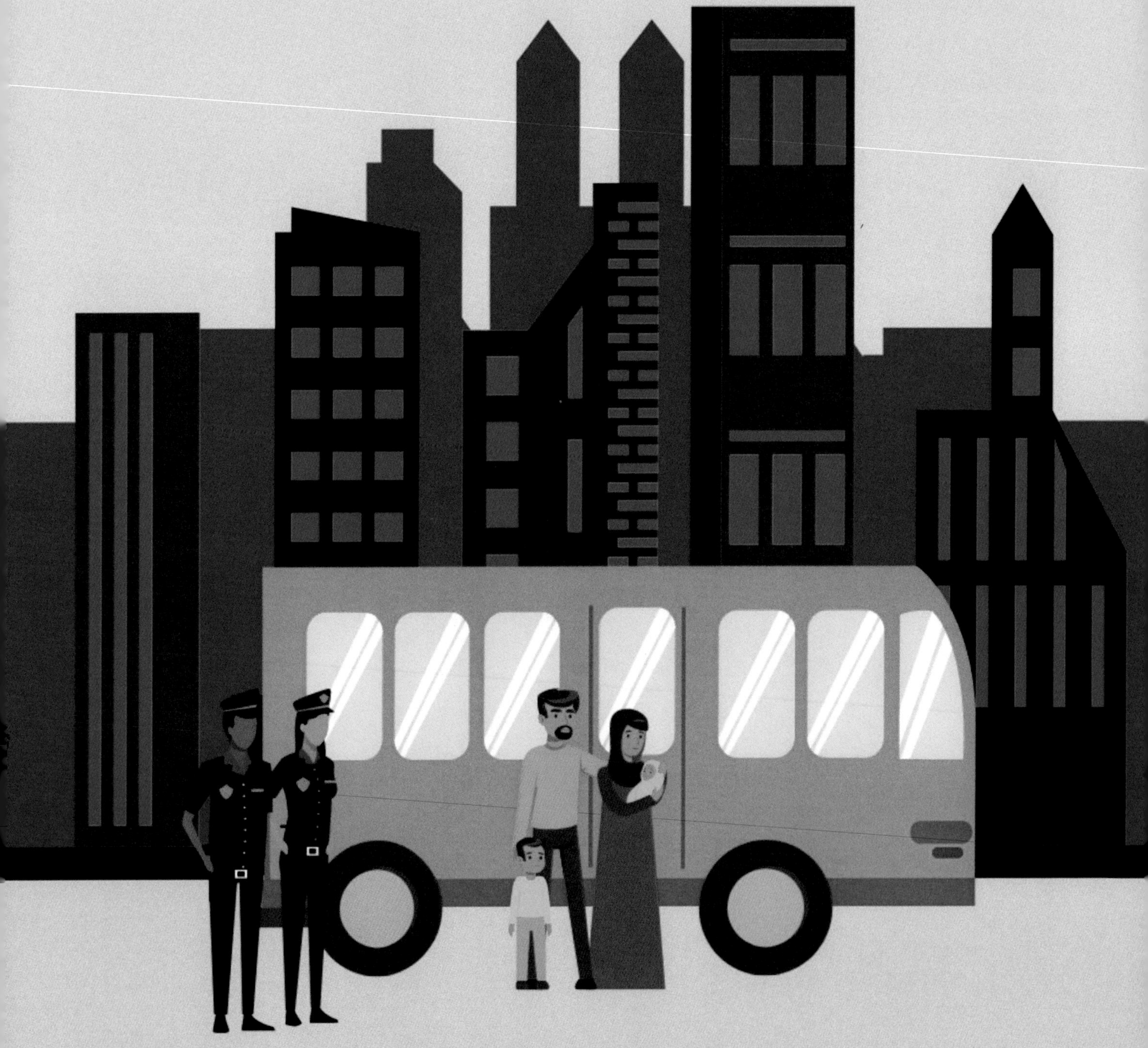

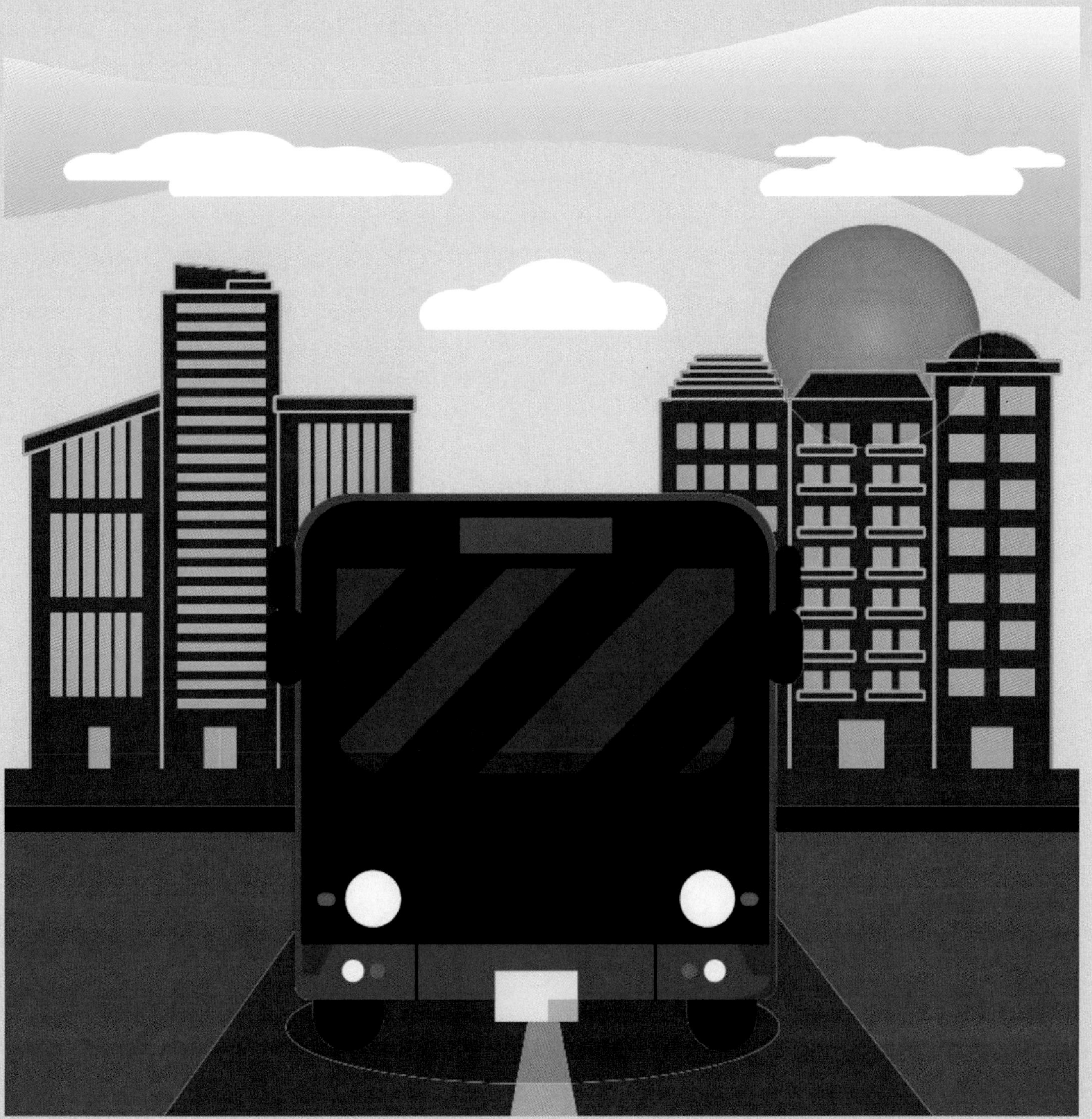

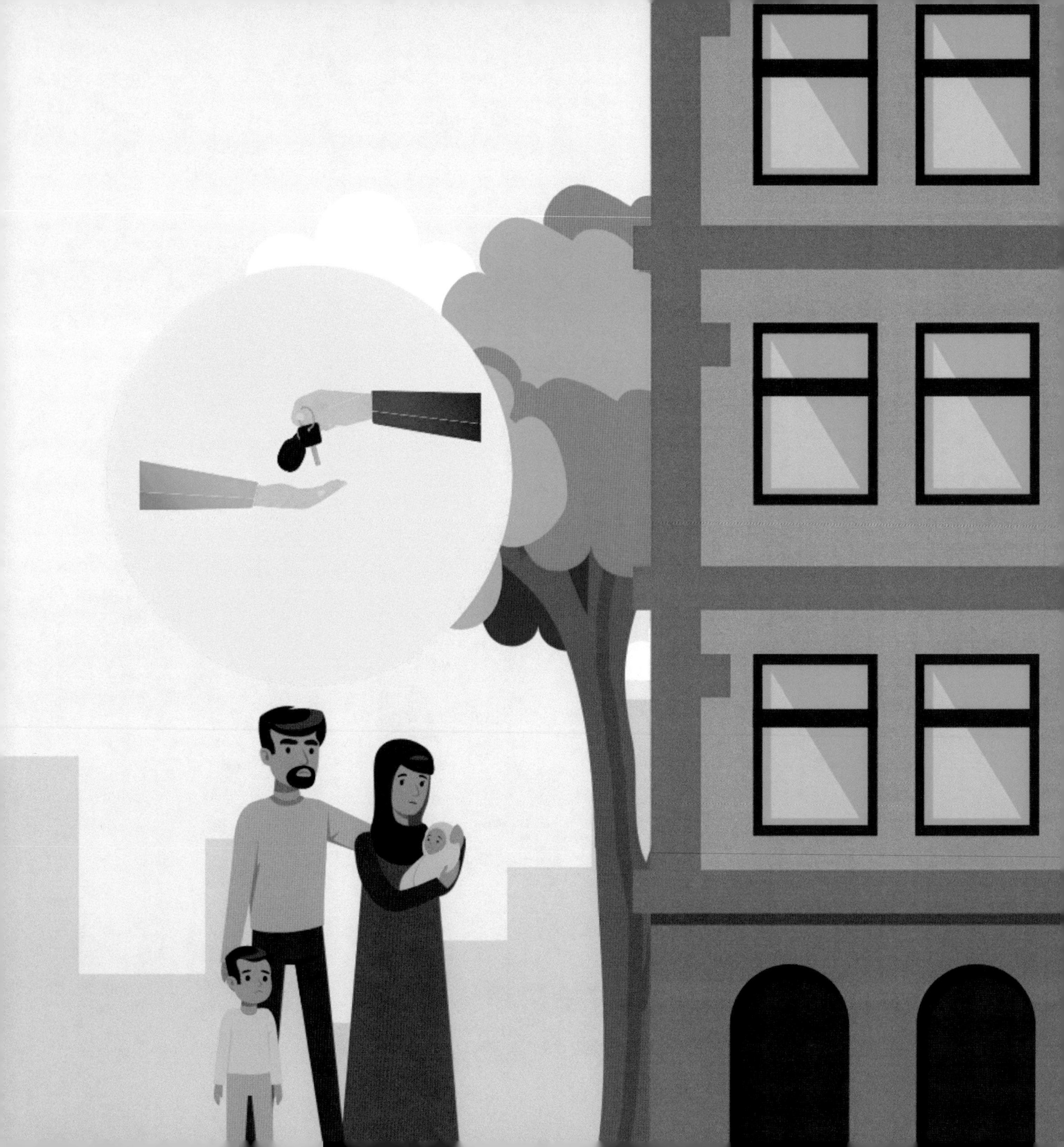

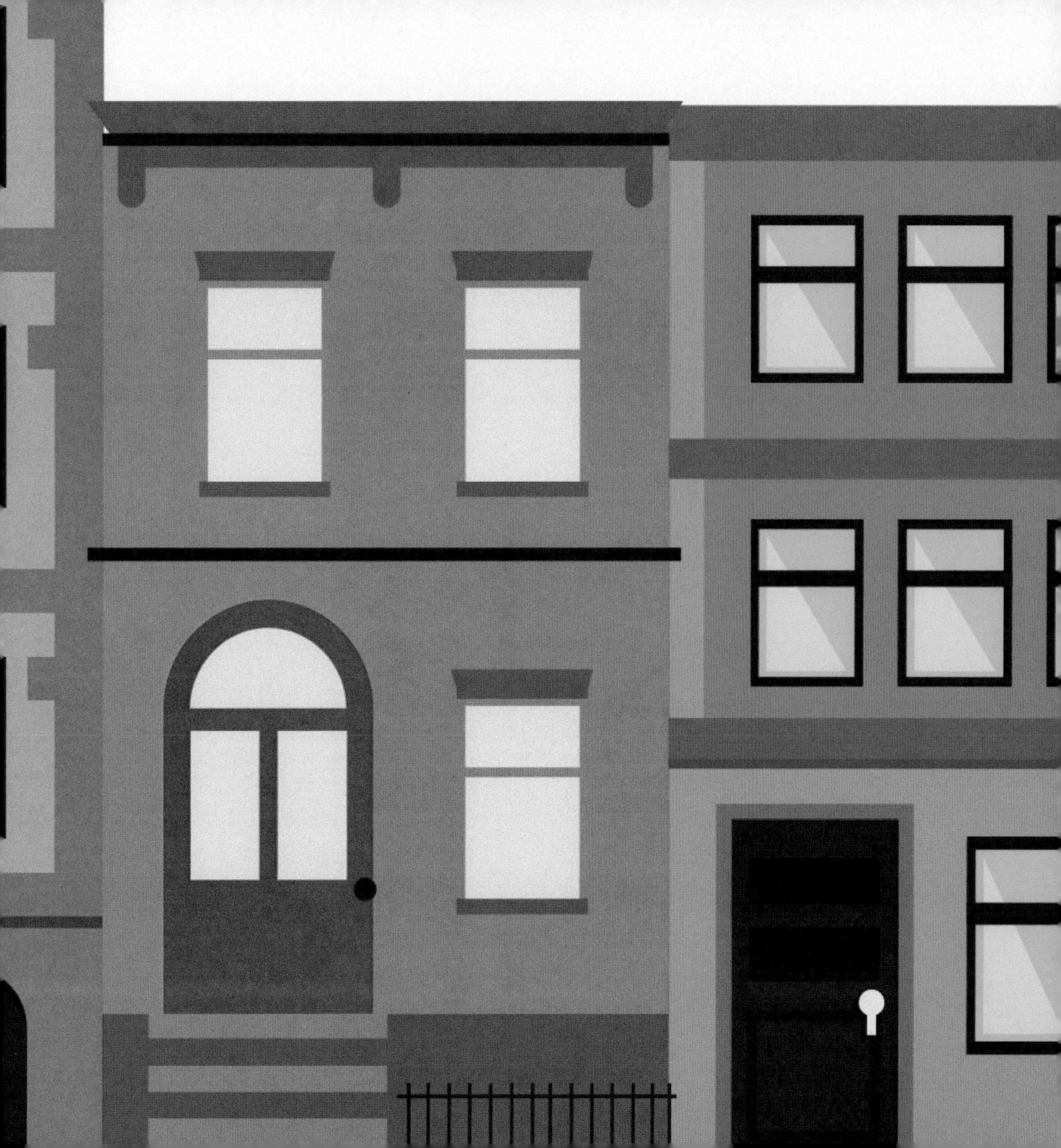

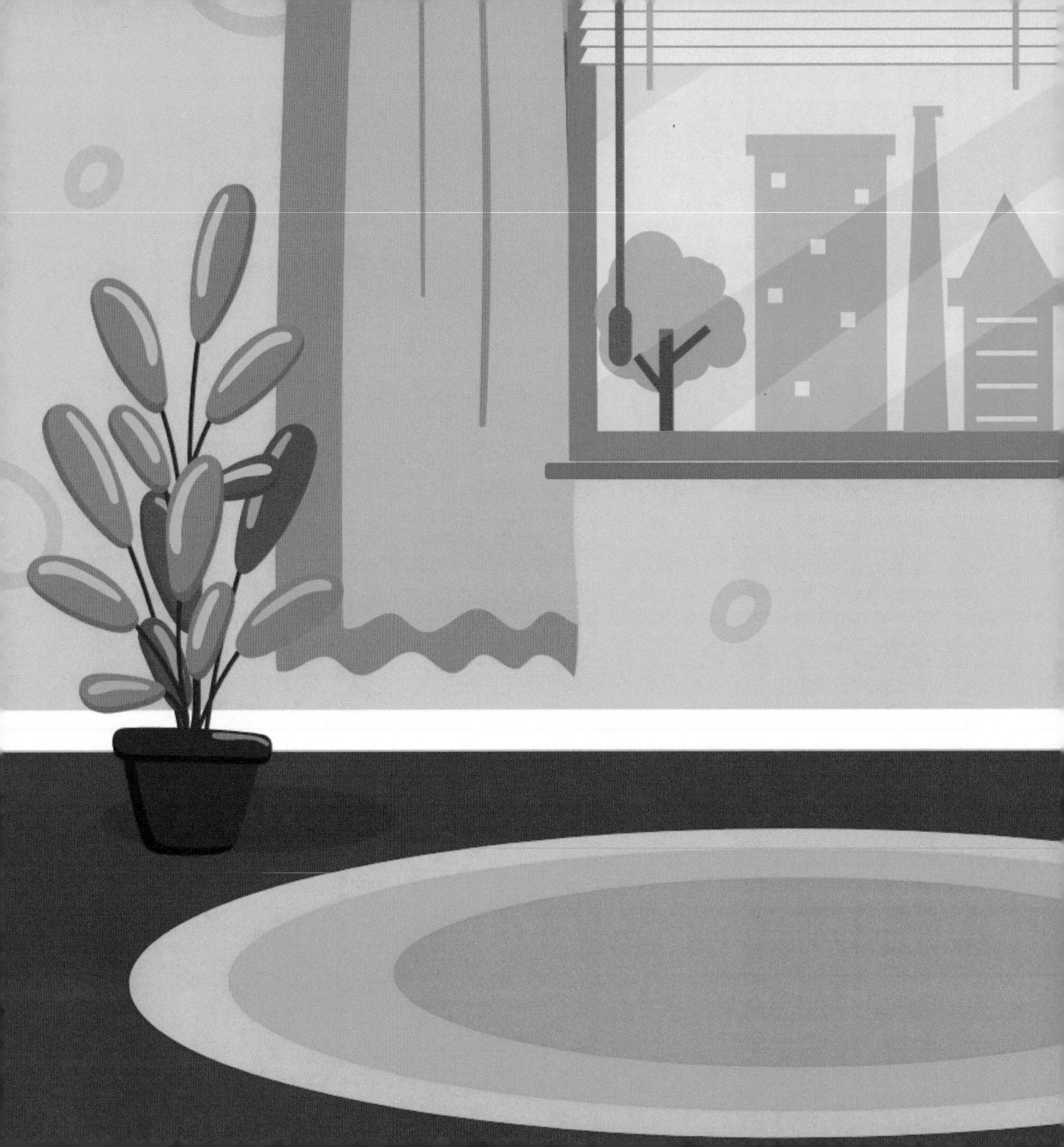

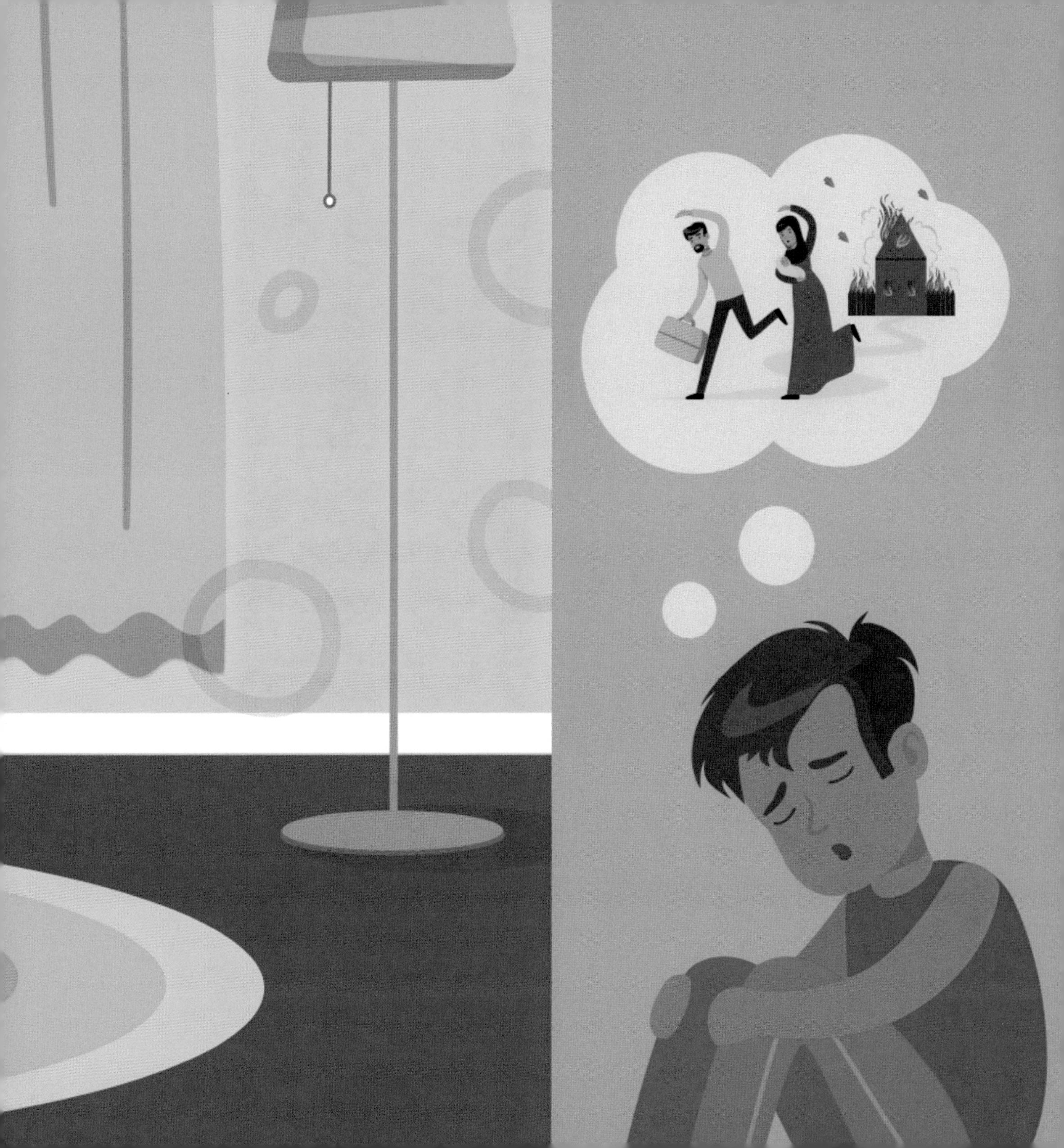

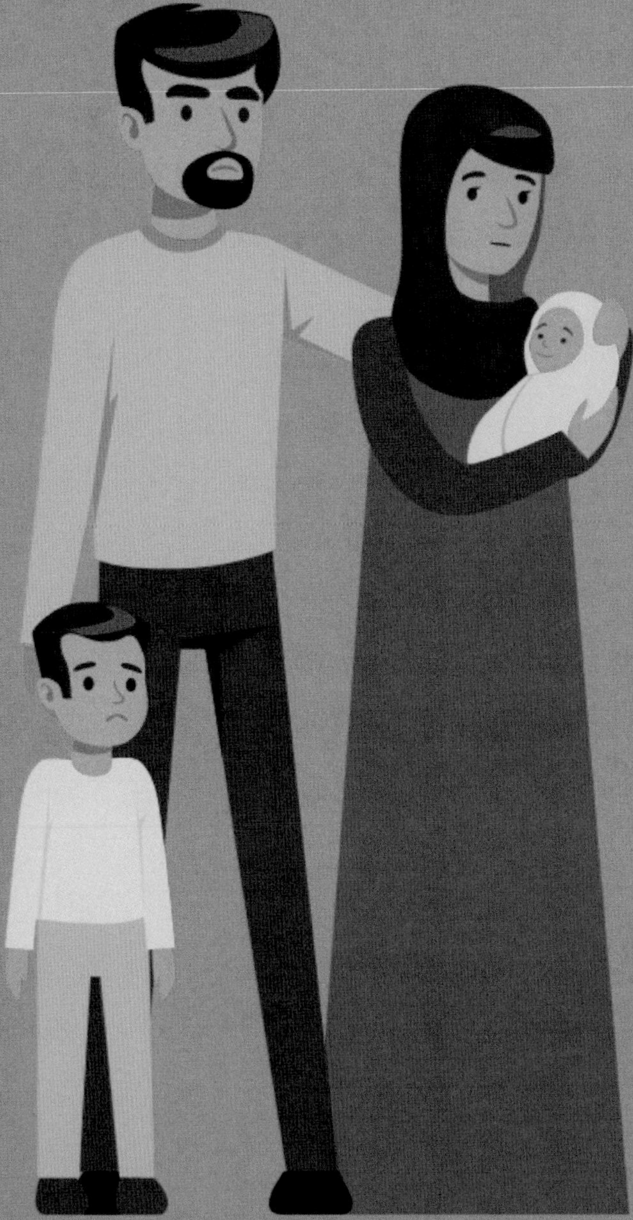

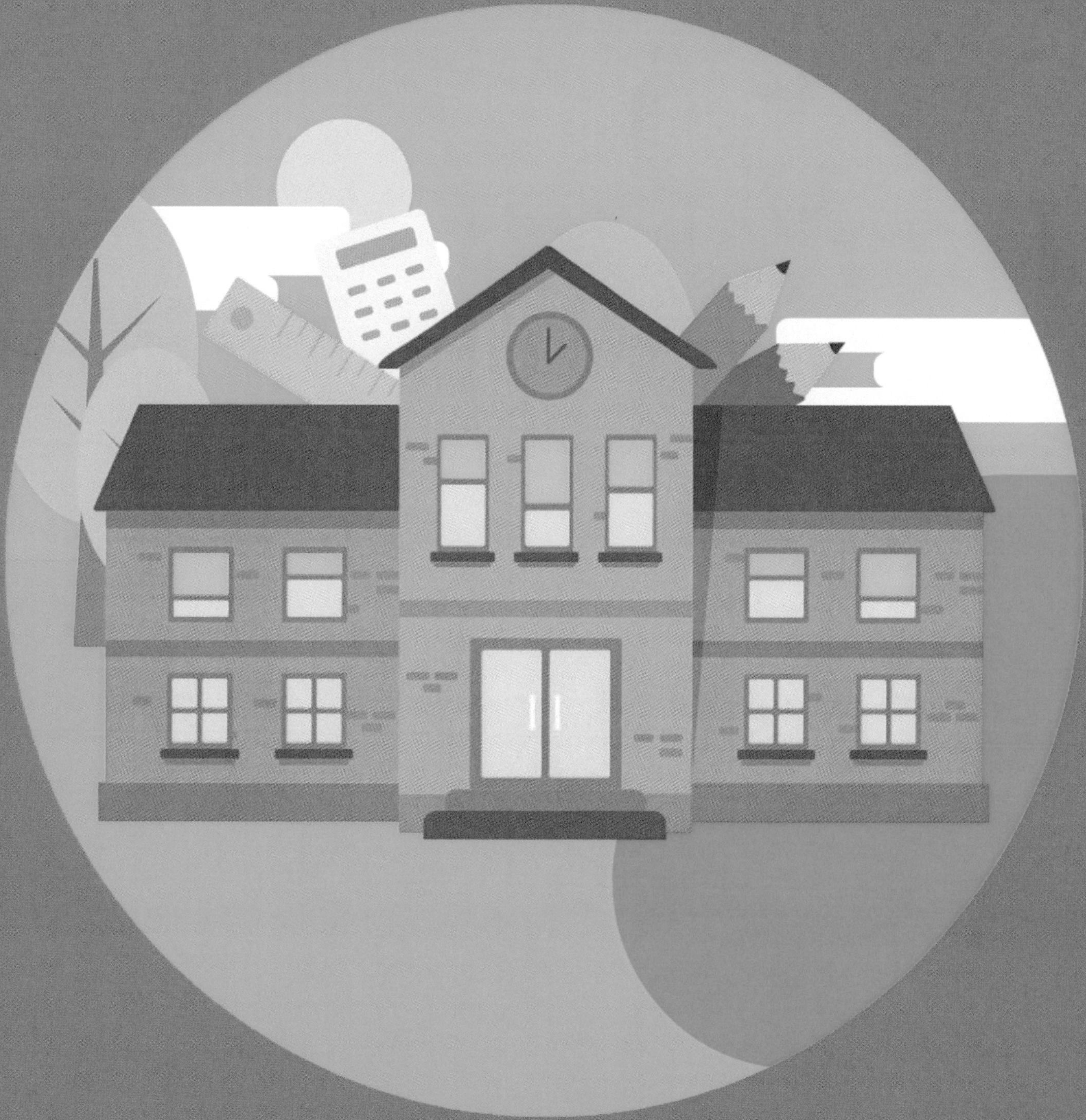

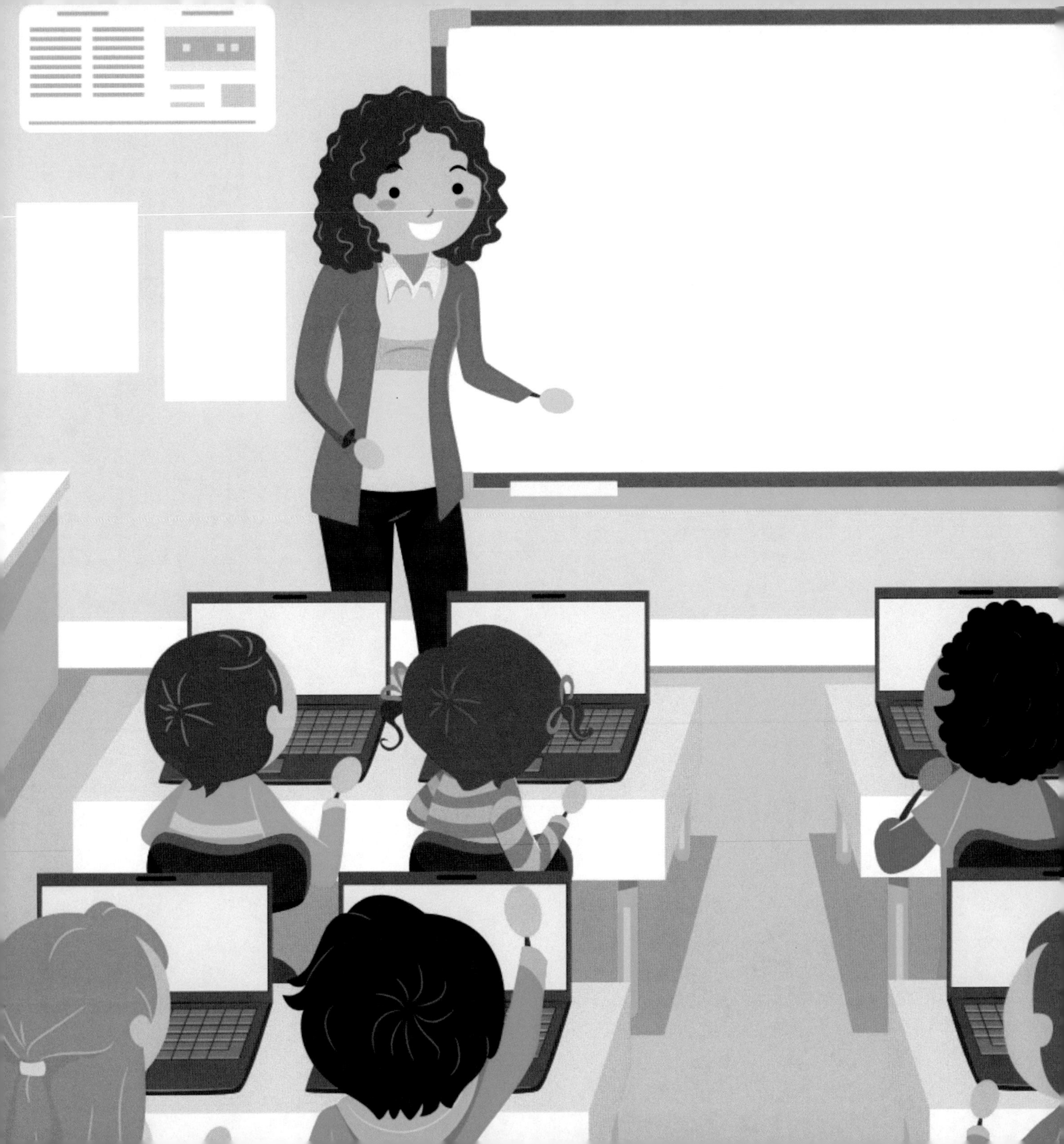

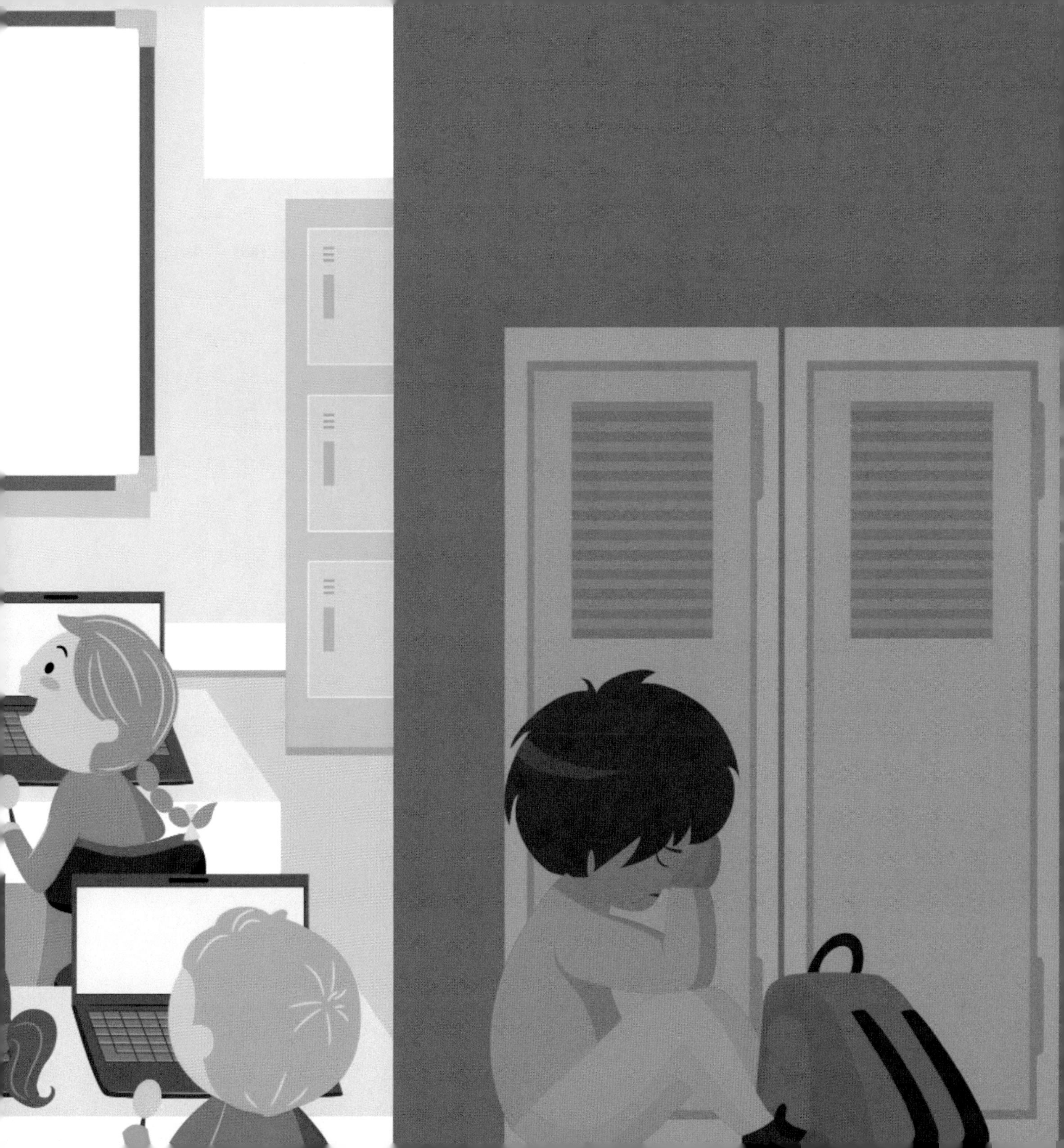

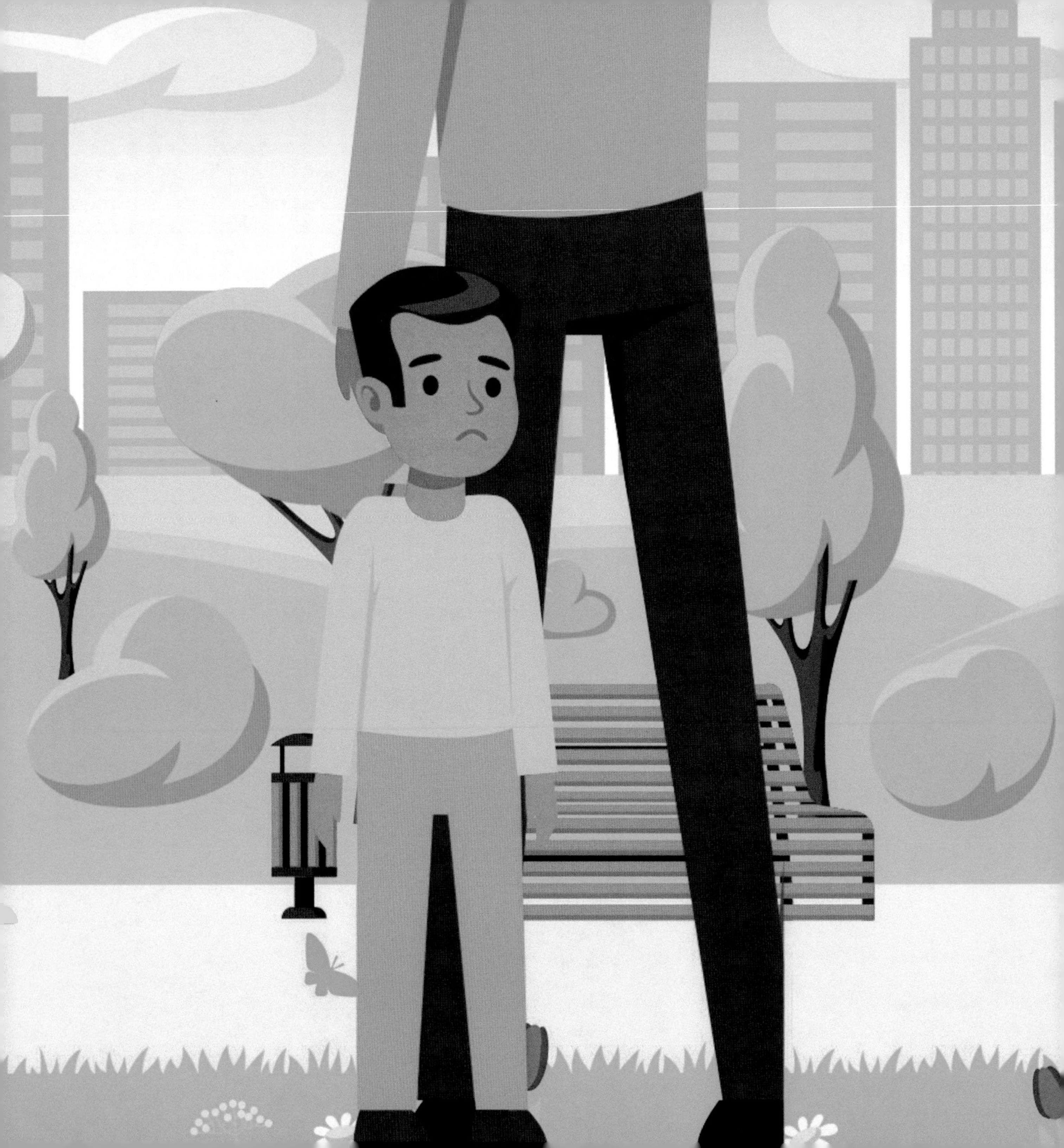

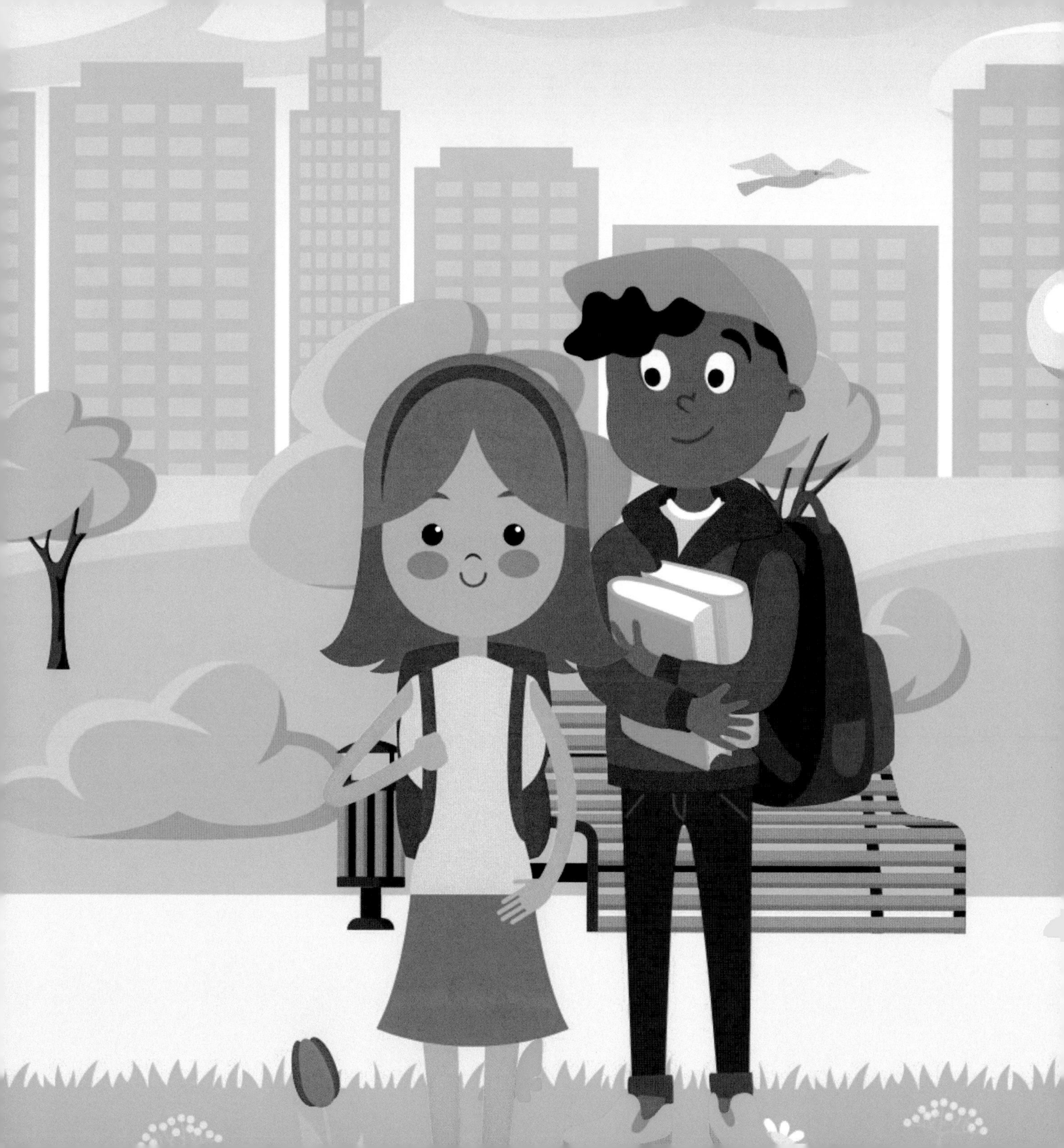

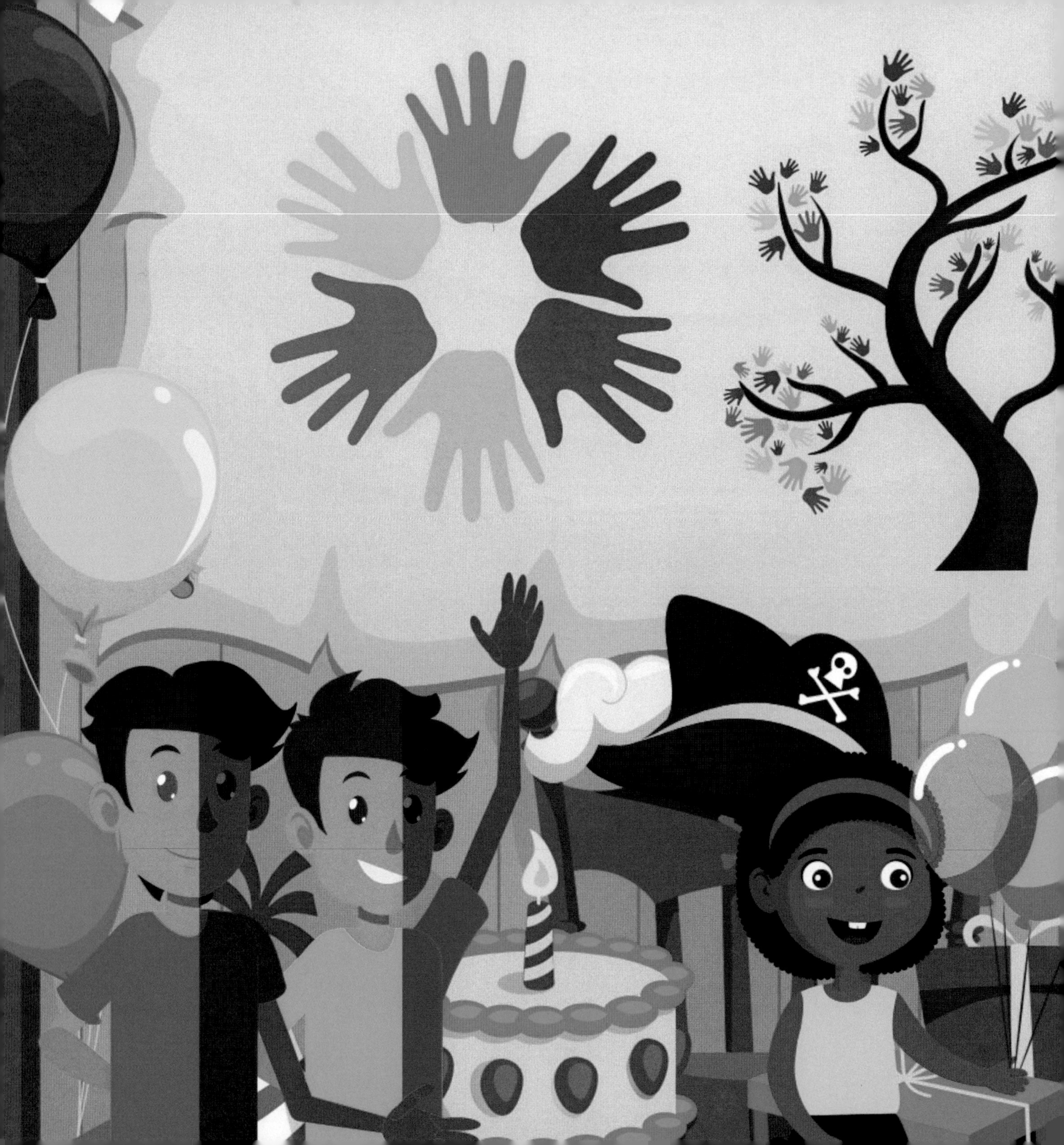

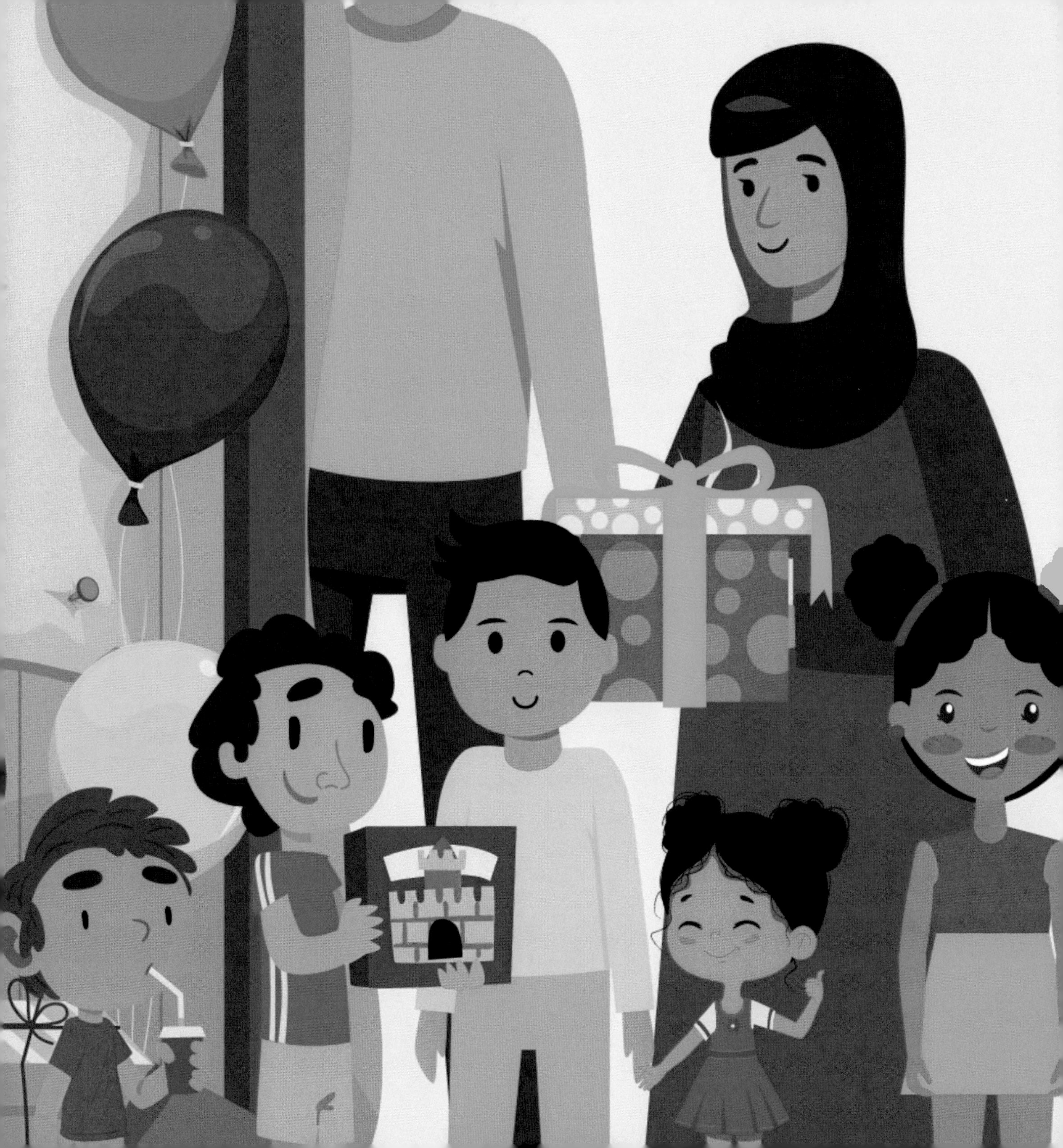

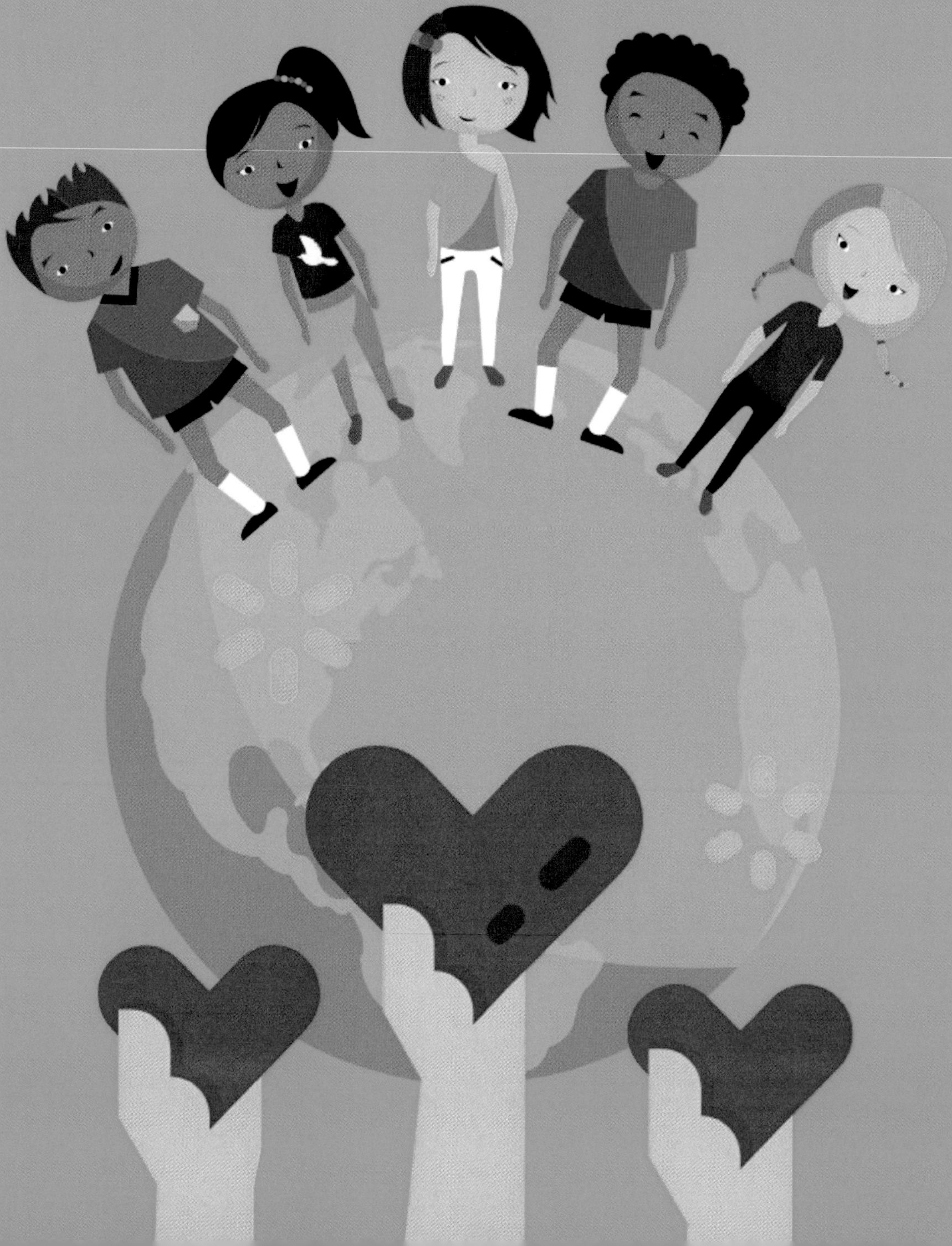

Three Famous Refugees

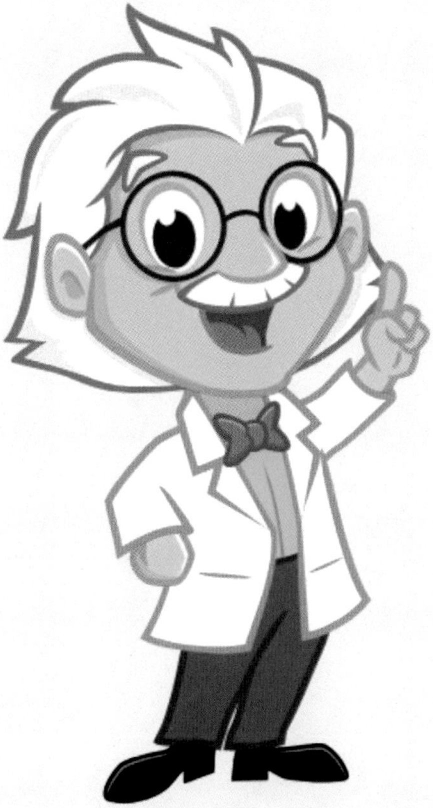

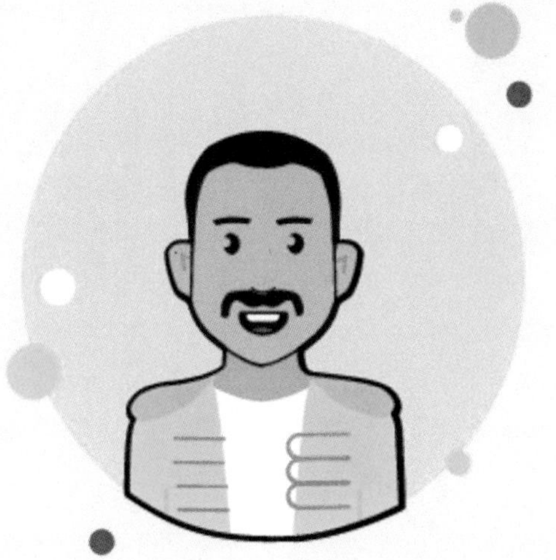

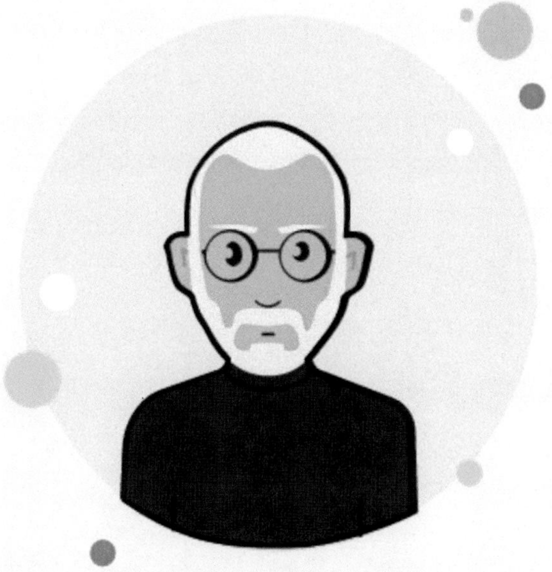

Made in the USA
Monee, IL
01 October 2024

67030472R00029